3|01

COUNTRIES OF THE WORLD

France

Gareth Stevens Publishing
MILWAUKEE

About the Author: Roseline NgCheong-Lum was born and raised in Mauritius, a former French colony. She has frequently traveled to France and is the author of several children's books.

Written by
ROSELINE NGCHEONG-LUM

Edited by
AYESHA ERCELAWN

Designed by
LOO CHUAN MING

Picture research by
SUSAN JANE MANUEL

First published in North America in 1999 by
Gareth Stevens Publishing
1555 North RiverCenter Drive, Suite 201
Milwaukee, Wisconsin 53212 USA

For a free color catalog describing
Gareth Stevens' list of high-quality books
and multimedia programs, call
1-800-542-2595 (USA) or
1-800-461-9120 (CANADA).
Gareth Stevens Publishing's
Fax: (414) 225-0377.
See our catalog, too, on the World Wide Web:
gsinc.com

© TIMES EDITIONS PTE LTD 1999
Originated and designed by
Times Books International
an imprint of Times Editions Pte Ltd
Times Centre, 1 New Industrial Road
Singapore 536196
http://www.timesone.com.sg/te

Library of Congress Cataloging-in-Publication Data
NgCheong-Lum, Roseline, 1962–
France / by Roseline NgCheong-Lum.
p. cm. -- (Countries of the world)
Includes bibliographical references and index.
Summary: An overview of France, discussing its history, geography, government, economy, culture, and relations with North America.
ISBN 0-8368-2260-9 (lib.bdg.)
1. France -- Juvenile literature. [1. France.] I. Title.
II. Series: Countries of the world (Milwaukee, Wis.)
DC33.N48   1999
944--dc21   98-33770

Printed in Singapore

1 2 3 4 5 6 7 8 9 03 02 01 00 99

Contents

AN OVERVIEW OF FRANCE

France, the largest country in Western Europe, has been a leader in the arts and political ideas for many centuries. The world still looks to France in matters of style and good taste, for the French have a reputation for elegance and refinement, which they demonstrate daily. They coined the phrase *joie de vivre*, which means "joy in living," and they try to enjoy every single day. Yet, France is also a country of sharp contrasts: between north and south, rich and poor, cities and countryside. Highly advanced technology exists side by side with handmade cheeses, the latest fashions in cities with traditional pastimes in villages, and the newest architectural designs with fine old buildings.

Opposite: **The charms of a small village in southwestern France. This peaceful region was once the site of frequent wars against the English and between Catholics and Protestants.**

Below: **Three children in their garden.**

THE FLAG OF FRANCE

The French flag is called the tricolor because of its three colors: blue, white, and red. It dates back to the French Revolution and became the national flag in 1794. The flag combines blue and red, the colors of the city of Paris, with the royal color white. Blue was the color of the Frankish kings whose kingdom centered around Paris. Charlemagne and his descendants rode to battle under a blue flag. Red was the color of medieval kings who used it in honor of Saint Denis, the first French saint. White was the color of the kings of France between 1638 and 1790. Today, all territories belonging to France use the tricolor flag.

Geography

The Land

France is sometimes called the Hexagon because of its six-sided shape. With a land area of 212,742 square miles (551,000 square kilometers), France is the largest country in Western Europe. It is the only country facing both the Atlantic Ocean and the Mediterranean Sea. Germany, Luxembourg, and Belgium are neighbors to the northeast, Italy and Switzerland to the east, and Spain to the south. Corsica, an island in the Mediterranean, is

also part of France, as are several territories scattered in the Caribbean Sea, the Pacific Ocean, the Indian Ocean, the Atlantic Ocean, and Antarctica.

The most striking geographical feature of France is the Massif Central, a huge granite plateau that covers one-sixth of the country. The area is dotted with extinct volcanoes, crater lakes, and hot springs, including the health spa of Vichy. Although the northwestern edge of the Massif is covered with green pastureland, most of the region is barren and thinly populated.

Paris, the capital city, is in the northern part of the country, a fertile agricultural area that has also developed a strong technology-based economy. In western France, the landscape

Above: **The French Alps stretch south from Lake Geneva almost to the Mediterranean Sea. They include the highest peak in France, Mont Blanc, which is also the highest mountain in Europe at 15,771 feet (4,805 meters).**

ranges from marshes to great pine forests. The Atlantic coast has large expanses of fine sandy beaches. The south of France has a good climate and fertile soil. Eastern France is dominated by the majestic snow-capped peaks of the Alps. The Rhône River flows through eastern France and is a vital link between north and south. France's second largest city, Lyon, was founded by the Romans on the banks of the Rhône.

The Pyrenees, in the south, act as a natural boundary between France and Spain. This mountain range extends from the Mediterranean Sea to the Atlantic coast. Many of its peaks rise up to 10,000 feet (3,050 m). The Pyrenees are lush and green on the

SAVING THE EARTH

He called it "the silent world," and through his fascinating underwater photography, Jacques-Yves Cousteau captured the world of the oceans and people's imaginations. France's most famous ecologist, Cousteau campaigned vigorously for the protection of marine life.

(A Closer Look, page 66)

French side, but arid and barren on the Spanish side. This region is the last remaining area of wilderness in southern Europe and supports many types of endangered wildlife.

Rivers

Rivers are an important means of communication between different regions. Most of France's cities have been built along the banks of rivers. Paris is on the Seine. Lyon lies at the point where the Rhône and Saône rivers meet. In the west, Bordeaux sits on the bank of the Garonne River. The longest river in France is the Loire, at 634 miles (1,020 km). The Rhine provides hydroelectricity to the regions of Alsace and Lorraine.

Above: **The Seine winds through northern France and flows into the English Channel near the port of Le Havre. Paris, the capital city, was founded on a small island in the middle of the river. The city of Rouen is also located along its banks.**

The Seasons

France has a predominantly temperate climate with mild winters, except in mountain areas and the northeast. The northwest is humid and experiences violent winds and heavy rains that blow in from the Atlantic Ocean. The south has a pleasant, Mediterranean climate. Summers are hot and winters mild. Spring and autumn downpours are sudden but brief. A peculiar feature is the *mistral* (miss-TRAHL), a cold, dry wind that blows in the spring and can reach speeds of 65 miles (105 km) per hour. The highest temperatures, over 90° Fahrenheit (32° Centigrade), are recorded on the Riviera, along the Mediterranean coast.

Left: **Winter in Alsace. The Alps and northeastern France have the coldest winters, with temperatures dipping to below freezing in January. The mountains receive the most rain, while the area around Paris is the driest.**

Plants and Animals

Woods and forests cover 26 percent of France's total area. Efforts by the National Forestry Office have increased total forested areas since 1945. Most trees are deciduous; only one-third are conifers. Oak and beech are common in the northern and central regions, while juniper and pine thrive in the Alps. Cypress, chestnut, and ash form thick forests in other parts of France. The south has orchards of citrus fruit trees as well as olive trees.

Forests and national parks are home to wild animals, such as brown bears, lynx, wolves, deer, and polecats. The Pyrenean bear is close to extinction, but the Pyrenean ibex, a type of antelope, is

still numerous in the mountains. Small mammals include beavers, hares, moles, badgers, rabbits, and squirrels. A variety of snakes live in forested areas, and the largest European lizard lives in the Luberon hills. The griffon vulture, which was nearly extinct early in the twentieth century, is now protected and has made a reappearance in the skies of the Cévennes highlands. This giant scavenger has a wingspan of 8 feet (2.4 m). The coastal areas support a variety of wildlife, from birds to fish and shellfish.

WILD HORSES, FLAMINGOS, AND GYPSIES

The Camargue marshlands in southern France have unique fauna and flora. They were declared a nature reserve in 1927 and support an incredible diversity of bird life, including flamingos, storks, and bee-eaters. Gypsies gather here once a year for a festival.
(*A Closer Look*, page 72)

Left: Storks live in the marshes of Alsace and have become that region's symbol. They migrate from Africa during the summer months and build nests of twigs and sticks in high places, including tall trees, rooftops, and church steeples. Breeding centers have also been set up because the birds' population is declining.

History

Gaul

France has been inhabited for more than forty thousand years. The first inhabitants were hunter-gatherers who lived an itinerant lifestyle. They were followed by the Cro-Magnon people, who appeared around 25,000 B.C. The Celts migrated to Gaul, as the country was then called, around 1200 B.C. and developed a complex society of warriors, farmers, artisans, and druids (medicine men).

The Romans began to invade Gaul in 200 B.C. When the Celtic leader, Vercingetorix, was defeated by Julius Caesar in 52 B.C., Gaul became a province of the Roman Empire. The province prospered, roads were built, and the Gauls converted to Christianity. Gaul remained under Roman control until the fifth century A.D. In the third century, however, as the Roman Empire declined, Franks and other Germanic tribes began to raid Gallic settlements, causing havoc in the towns and villages.

Below: **The defeated Celtic leader, Vercingetorix, lays down his arms before Julius Caesar.**

The Middle Ages

Frankish tribes from Germany began to settle in Gaul in the region around Paris and soon took over the country from the Romans. Clovis became king in 481, and the country was renamed France. He chose Paris as his capital and converted to Christianity. Power struggles, betrayals, and conspiracies made the sixth to eighth centuries a very unstable period until Charlemagne, king of the Carolingian dynasty (a Frankish dynasty named for its many kings who were called Charles), united the country in 768. Charlemagne extended his territory and became Holy Roman Emperor in 800. Later, Hugh Capet founded the Capetian dynasty, which ruled France for the rest of the Middle Ages. It was a time of prosperity and scholastic achievement. French noblemen were involved in the Crusades, which tried to wrest control of Jerusalem, the Christian Holy Land, from the Muslims.

In 1337, France became involved in a drawn-out series of wars with the English. The Hundred Years' War, as this series of wars is known, finally ended with the defeat of the English in 1453.

THE SUN KING

Said to radiate light and glory like the sun, Louis XIV was one of the greatest kings of France.
(A Closer Look, page 68)

Renaissance France

The Renaissance came to France via Italy when the French invaded that country in 1494. By 1500, the boundaries of France were, more or less, what they are today. Francis I, who ruled from 1515 to 1547, was a true Renaissance prince. He brought well-known Italian artists and musicians to his court, including Leonardo da Vinci and Benvenuto Cellini. Under his patronage, the arts flourished in France.

The sixteenth century, however, also saw increasing religious wars. Protestantism had spread across France, and struggles between Catholics and Protestants, or Huguenots, grew. Henry IV of Navarre, born Protestant, became Catholic for the sake of peace when he succeeded to the throne, but he showed considerable religious tolerance to the Protestants.

The seventeenth century saw another great king, Louis XIV, the Sun King. He fought Germany and Italy to strengthen the territorial holdings of France. He also encouraged the French exploration of North America, and supported an even greater outpouring of art than Francis I. His extravagances, however, depleted the treasury of the country and led to the public dissatisfaction that would culminate in the French Revolution.

MAID OF ORLÉANS

France was embroiled in the Hundred Years' War with England from 1337 to 1453. English attempts at invasion were repelled when Joan of Arc led the French army to victory. Unfortunately, she was later captured and burned at the stake.
(A Closer Look, page 60)

The French Revolution

By the late 1780s, the peasants, the bourgeoisie, and the nobles all had strong reasons for being unhappy with King Louis XVI and his wife, Marie Antoinette. Spurred by the ideas of Enlightenment philosophers on social justice and by the success of the American Revolution, the population staged an uprising against the monarchy. On July 14, 1789, a Parisian mob stormed the Bastille prison. The storming of the Bastille is considered the start of the French Revolution. The royal family was arrested, and the king and queen were beheaded in 1793. The Reign of Terror followed, in which thousands of people were put to death. Order was established only in 1799, when Napoleon Bonaparte took power. After a series of wars, France controlled most of Western Europe. Bonaparte was crowned Emperor Napoleon I but was ultimately defeated by the armies allied against him. His nephew later became Napoleon III and proceeded to modernize the country. After Napoleon III abdicated in 1871, France became a republic.

Above: **Peasants as well as the urban masses rose up against the aristocracy during the French Revolution. Many castles were stormed, and peasants destroyed the records of their debts.**

DEADLY INVENTION

The guillotine became infamous after the French Revolution, when it was used to execute hundreds of people.
(A Closer Look, page 50)

The Twentieth Century

By the beginning of the twentieth century, France was a strong colonial power with territories in Africa, Indochina, and the central and south Pacific Ocean. It had started building a colonial empire in the eighteenth century, declaring its first colonies in North America — New France (Quebec) and Louisiana. By the nineteenth century, however, France had lost both colonies, Quebec to Britain and Louisiana in a sale to the United States, called the Louisiana Purchase. France then turned toward Africa and Asia, bringing most of north and west Africa under French rule and also colonizing Indochina and many islands in the Pacific and Indian oceans and in the Caribbean.

In 1904, the Entente Cordiale ended colonial rivalry between France and Britain in Africa and began a period of cooperation that has continued to this day. In 1907, France joined with Britain and Russia to check Germany's expansionist ideas. The Germans, however, were not deterred, and invaded France at the beginning of World War I (1914–1918). Much of that war was fought on French soil, and France suffered heavy casualties. Altogether, two million French soldiers died in the war.

When the United States entered the war in 1917, it helped the French defeat the German army and win back the regions of Alsace and Lorraine, which Germany had taken in the Franco-Prussian War in 1870.

THE FOUR CORNERS OF THE WORLD

After losing its American colonies, France started to colonize north and west Africa. Vietnam, Laos, and Cambodia, in Asia, became part of French Indochina. Islands in the Pacific and Indian oceans, as well as in the Caribbean, were also colonized. Today, only a few small overseas territories remain in French control.

(A Closer Look, page 54)

Left: **The Arc de Triomphe in Paris was first commissioned by Napoleon I to commemorate his victories. Later, the victorious Allies triumphantly marched through the arch after World Wars I and II. The body of an Unknown Soldier is buried underneath the arch, and a national remembrance is held there every year.**

13

World War II

After World War I, France depended greatly on German war payments to rebuild the country. When Germany stopped the payments and Nazi leader Adolf Hitler invaded Poland, in 1939, France joined Britain in declaring war on Germany, and World War II (1939–1945) began. In 1940, the Germans invaded Paris and occupied the northern and western parts of France. They installed a government for the south, in Vichy, under Marshal Pétain. Although French in name, the Vichy government was actually German-controlled. The French people never recognized the legitimacy of the puppet government, and those who collaborated with the German army were lynched in public. Many who opposed the Nazis formed an underground resistance movement led by General Charles de Gaulle, who had been under-secretary of war at the outbreak of World War II. De Gaulle fled to London and established a government-in-exile. The French Resistance fighters gathered information for the Allied forces and also waged guerrilla warfare against German soldiers. France was liberated in 1944 when Allied forces, made up of British, American, and Canadian soldiers, landed on the beaches of Normandy. De Gaulle returned to Paris and set up a new government.

Above: **Charles de Gaulle (1890–1970).**

Post-War France

The post-war years were characterized by strong economic and technological progress in France, although the country lost most of its colonies in Africa and Indochina. Charles de Gaulle marked the 1950s and 1960s with his dominating presence. He had a vision for France and was determined to turn the country into the leader of Europe. He strongly favored a European Union but was adamantly against membership for Britain.

The most striking event of the post-war years was a series of student demonstrations in 1968. Starting on the campus of the University of Paris, the movement soon involved blue-collar workers in a show of dissatisfaction against the government and existing social norms. The country came to a standstill, and the de Gaulle government was almost overthrown. However, good sense prevailed, and the government brought sweeping reforms to many sectors of French society. In the 1980s and 1990s, a new phenomenon, "cohabitation," appeared in French politics, with the president and the government belonging to different political parties.

CHARLES DE GAULLE

One of France's greatest war heroes was Charles de Gaulle. Opposing the Nazi-installed French government during World War II, de Gaulle fled to London in 1940 and organized the Free French forces. His regular radio broadcasts helped the Resistance movement oust the Nazis. After the war, de Gaulle was elected provisional president of France. He resigned a year later, however, because he felt the constitution did not give enough power to the president. In 1958, a new constitution that strengthened the presidency was written, and in 1959, de Gaulle became president of the new republic.

Charlemagne (742–814)

Charlemagne became king of France in 768. At that time, Europe was in turmoil. Charlemagne was determined to bring back civilization and order. In 800, he was named the emperor of Western Europe. His vast realm included what is now France, Switzerland, Belgium, and the Netherlands, half of present-day Italy and Germany, and parts of Austria, as well as Spain.

Charlemagne placed great importance on education and established the first educational institution at Aix-la-Chapelle. For this reason, French children like to sing that "old Charlemagne invented school!" He was a tireless reformer who tried to improve people's lives.

Charlemagne

Marie Antoinette (1755–1793)

Marie Antoinette, an Austrian, was queen of France at the time of the Revolution. It was rumored that, when told the people were so poor they did not even have bread to eat, she retorted they should eat cake instead! These words so angered the citizens of Paris that they decided to do away with the monarchy. She was hated for not making an effort to understand the people and for frivolously spending money. Marie Antoinette never looked on France as her country, and the French considered her a foreigner, calling her "the Austrian woman." She was executed by guillotine in 1793.

Marie Antoinette

Napoleon Bonaparte (1769–1821)

Napoleon Bonaparte was born on the island of Corsica. He was a military genius who efficiently brought order back to France after the Revolution. He embarked on a series of wars to conquer most of Western Europe and crowned himself emperor in 1804. Defeated at Waterloo in 1815, he was exiled by the British to the island of Saint Helena in the South Atlantic. He died there in 1821.

Napoleon is also remembered for collecting and revising French laws into codes. The most famous of these, the Code Napoléon, or Code Civil, still forms the basis of French civil law. Napoleon also founded the Bank of France and centralized France's government.

Napoleon Bonaparte

Government and the Economy

When the French Revolution overthrew the monarchy in 1789, France became one of the first republics in the world. Its republican system is divided into three branches: the executive branch made up of the president, the prime minister, and a cabinet of ministers; the legislative branch, consisting of the National Assembly and the Senate; and the judicial branch, a system of courts of justice.

The president is the head of state and is elected for a seven-year term. He appoints the prime minister from the largest party in the National Assembly. While the prime minister sees to the day-to-day running of the country, the president focuses on national and foreign policy.

Jacques Chirac *(far left)* was elected president of the country in 1995 for a seven-year term. Lionel Jospin *(left)* became prime minister in 1997.

Provincial Administration

France is divided into twenty-two regions, which are further divided into ninety-six departments. Local government deals mainly with town planning and urban development. Each department has a main town and is run by a local council. Councilors are elected in local elections. A commissioner represents the central government.

The smallest administrative unit is the commune, or township. There are 36,500 communes throughout France, ranging from small villages to large cities. The head of a commune is the mayor, who is elected by the local municipal council.

Voting

All persons over eighteen years old are allowed to vote. Voting is not compulsory, but elections generally witness a healthy turn-out. French voters take part in presidential, National Assembly, Senate, and European Union elections. They also vote for their local councils.

Presidential elections are carried out over two rounds. Any number of candidates can run for office in the first round. The second round, about a week later, is between the two candidates who received the highest number of votes in the first round. The presidential election always ends up as a confrontation between Left and Right parties, because parties whose candidates were defeated in the first round give their support to the candidate whose ideology is closest to theirs in the second round.

National Service

All men between the ages of eighteen and thirty-five are called up for one year of national service in the army, navy, or air force. The government is discussing changing this system, however, and is contemplating a professional army instead of compulsory service.

COHABITATION

Presidential elections are held separately from legislative elections, which leads to the phenomenon of "cohabitation." This occurs when the president and prime minister are from different sides of the political spectrum. First, Socialist president François Mitterrand was forced to "cohabit" with rightist Prime Minister Jacques Chirac. In 1997, the roles were reversed: Jacques Chirac as president had to govern with a Socialist prime minister, Lionel Jospin.

Natural Resources

France's most important natural resource is its fertile soil. One-third of the land is under cultivation, and France is the second largest exporter of agricultural products in the world. It is also the leading producer and exporter of farm products in Europe. Agricultural output is high thanks to modern technology and substantial state subsidies. Nearly one million people work in the farming industry.

The main crops are wheat, corn, sugar beets, and grapes for the wine industry. French wines are considered among the best in the world. More than one-fifth of the land is devoted to pastures for grazing. Cattle are raised for milk production as well as meat. French dairy products, such as milk, cheese, and cream, are also among the finest in the world. France is the largest exporter of beef and veal in Western Europe.

Iron ore and bauxite are the two most significant minerals in France. They are turned into steel and aluminum sheets, which are used extensively in industry. Coal is also mined, together with zinc and potash. Mining, however, is in decline in France, as in other industrialized countries.

A NOSE FOR PERFUMES

It takes a special person to become a "nose" in the perfume industry. He or she must be able to identify one scent among six thousand!
(*A Closer Look, page 64*)

Below: In coastal areas, such as Brittany, fish are an abundant natural resource and an important part of the economy. French trawlers and smaller boats catch tuna, sardines, and anchovies in inland coastal waters. They also venture to Africa and the waters of Iceland and Newfoundland.

Major Industries

France is the fourth largest economic power in the world and a leading producer of industrial goods. The industrial sector generates one-quarter of the annual gross domestic product, and it is one of the most highly developed in the world. One-third of the labor force works in industry.

France has long been a successful manufacturer of luxury goods such as perfumes and textiles, and high fashion still brings in substantial revenue. The country is also gaining a strong reputation for manufacturing high technology goods. High-speed trains, jet fighters, satellites, cars, and telecommunications equipment top the list of industrial production. The Concorde and TGV train are the best examples of French technological achievements. The pharmaceutical sector accounts for an important section of industrial output, too. French laboratories are among the most advanced in the world, and scientific research into cures for diseases such as AIDS and cancer has top priority.

Below: Vineyards, like these, stretch through many parts of France. The grapes are harvested in the late summer and fall.

Trade

France trades mainly with countries in the European Union, especially Germany. Other large trading partners are the United States, Japan, and Russia. The country's primary exports are machinery, foodstuffs, chemicals, textiles, and iron and steel products. Crude oil is a major import, along with industrial equipment and agricultural products.

People and Lifestyle

France has a population of over fifty-eight million people, with slightly more women than men. It has a varied population, reflecting the different tribes that settled in France. People in the northern part of the country tend to be of Slavic or Teutonic ancestry, with fair hair and blue eyes. Southerners are of smaller build and darker in coloring, much like other peoples in the Mediterranean region.

Indigenous ethnic minorities include the Celts of Brittany, the Catalans of Languedoc-Roussillon, the Provençals of Provence, the Corsicans of Corsica, and the Basques of the Pyrenees.

In recent decades, especially after France's colonies were granted independence, many immigrants have come to add variety to the French population. The largest immigrant group in France is made up of North Africans from Algeria, Morocco, and Tunisia. Called *Beurs* (BURR), they form pockets of settlement in the large cities, especially in Marseille. Another large immigrant group is Indochinese, from Vietnam and Cambodia.

Above: **Two friends play on the sidewalk. France has a diversity of people, and many North Africans have immigrated to France from former colonies.**

Social Classes and Customs

Although France has been a republic for more than two hundred years, it is still a very hierarchical society. Social class dictates to a large extent the types of schools children attend, as well as their leisure activities and intellectual pursuits. French aristocracy is still alive, and nobles have retained their titles and many social privileges, in addition to great wealth.

The middle class is called the bourgeoisie. The majority of the population belongs to this class. They benefit from the best education available, and most French politicians come from the bourgeoisie. Lower-middle-class people are employed as teachers, office workers, and technicians. The working class, farmers and manual workers, is roughly one-third of the population. Most immigrant communities are considered lower class even though some members are successful professionals.

Because French society is so hierarchical, formality dominates every aspect of life. People greet each other by their last names and titles. Only among close friends do people use first names. A formal pronoun, *vous* (VOO), or "you," is used when addressing another person. The informal you, *tu* (TEU), is reserved for children, family members, and close friends. Young people are more casual about social relationships and use first names and *tu* more often.

Below: Families spend much of their free time together, often in outdoor activities such as picnics.

Left: A father and son harvest hay in the Pyrenees in July.

Rural Life

Rural lifestyles vary from region to region. Some families have owned their houses for generations. Many people, however, have moved to the towns and return to their village homes on weekends or during vacations.

The life of the village is centered on the village square, which is usually surrounded by a small church and a few essential shops. There is at least one bakery and a café in every village. In the evenings and on weekends, people may gather at the café to have a drink or, particularly in southern France, to watch the older men play a game of *boules* (BOOL) in the square.

Life in the country is slow and quiet, with the pattern broken once a week by the outdoor market. Yet, villages benefit from all types of modern amenities, such as cable television and Minitel (an online service much like the Internet). Most households own at least one car and a full range of electrical appliances.

City Life

Urban lifestyle in cities such as Paris and Lyon is not much different from other Western cities, such as New York or Los Angeles. The city center usually has elegant old buildings, once the houses of rich merchants and aristocrats. These structures have been converted into offices or tiny apartments with high rents. Although some are several stories high, very few have elevators, and most are occupied by couples without children or by single people who work in the city center. French zoning laws are very strict and have been effective in

keeping the character of older city centers. More than half of the urban population lives in the suburbs surrounding the cities, often in ugly apartment blocks called HLM (*habitations à loyer modéré*, or low-rent housing). Despite the social problems encountered in HLM blocks (drugs, gangs, and prostitution), they are the only form of housing which the low-income families can afford. Many city-dwellers maintain a second home in the countryside, usually in the village of their family. They escape the hustle and bustle of city living every weekend and come back refreshed.

Above: Paris is home to more than two million people.

THE CITY OF LIGHTS

Paris, the capital of France, is well known for its fashionable shops, sidewalk cafés, exceptional museums, and for being an intellectual and artistic wellspring of ideas. Those who visit fall in love with the city, and many who live there think it is the most beautiful city in the world.

(*A Closer Look, page 48*)

Family Life

Family ties are strong in France. Most families tend to be rather small, with one or two children, especially in the cities. French children see their grandparents and cousins on Sundays and during summer vacations. The children are usually well-behaved and learn good manners at a young age.

Women

Only in the last thirty years have French women won legal equality with men. They were granted the right to vote in 1945, but until 1965, husbands were considered the legal heads-of-household, and wives had to ask their permission to get a job. Hubertine Auclert was one of the first women to fight for women's rights in the late nineteenth century. She led marches, founded two feminist organizations, edited the first French suffragist newspaper, and was brought to trial for disrupting a polling place during elections in 1908. The first woman prime minister, Edith Cresson, was appointed in 1991. Although the French government has several women ministers, women overall are poorly represented in politics. In the workplace, too, few women have made it to the top. In French society, a successful businesswoman may even be viewed with slight contempt.

Above: **Marie and Pierre Curie.**

Education

The French government provides free and compulsory education for all children between the ages of six and sixteen. From ages two to six, French children go to preschool, where they learn to read.

Left: **More and more women in France are working, but few have made it into politics, and average salaries are lower than those of men.**

Preschool is followed by six years of primary school. When children are eleven years old, they go to secondary school, called *collége* (kol-EHJ), for four years. The top students continue for another three years of *lycée* (li-SAY) to prepare for the baccalaureate exams. About 75 percent of all students qualify to take these tough exams. Successful candidates go on to universities or *grandes écoles* (GRAN-dzay-KOHL), elite schools that are particularly strong in the technical and engineering fields.

Since the French Revolution, there has been a clear separation between the state and the church. Muslim girls wearing a head scarf may be expelled from school because they are considered to be flaunting their religion. Some parents prefer to send their children to private schools run by the Catholic Church.

In general, French children have little time to devote to extracurricular activities because they have a heavy workload at school. The school system is very competitive, and only the very bright students make it to the top. Sports, such as soccer, are the main extracurricular activities.

Above: **Extracurricular activities include music, gymnastics, soccer, scouting, or hobby clubs, such as stamp collecting.**

Religion

Nearly 90 percent of the French population is Christian, although most do not attend church on a regular basis. Many people still consult a priest, however, for important events in their lives, and are baptized, married, and buried by the church. Roman Catholicism is the main religion. Devout Catholics make pilgrimages to miraculous sites. Lourdes is one particularly well-visited shrine where people pray to the Virgin Mary.

Baptism and first communion are still very important rites of passage, especially in the countryside. Ceremonies are held in a church, then the extended family gathers for an elaborate meal, either in a café or at home. The meal always ends with a cake covered with white icing to symbolize the child's purity.

Long viewed as being rigid and distant, the Catholic Church has made tremendous efforts to get closer to the people. Many ceremonial traditions have been abandoned, and worship has been simplified to meet the needs of modern society. Services are now in French rather than Latin. Few priests wear a cassock when

Above: **A Catholic woman lights candles in Notre Dame Cathedral in Paris.**

MONT-SAINT-MICHEL

The massive abbey on the island of Mont-Saint-Michel dates back to the eleventh century and was founded by Benedictine monks.
(A Closer Look, page 62)

they are not conducting a service, and some even hold other jobs. The Catholic Church sees its role as providing pastoral care, that is, tending to the spiritual needs of the people, especially the young. It is very active in the fight against poverty and the rehabilitation of drug addicts.

Calvinist Protestants are the main non-Catholic Christians. Their name comes from Jean Calvin, a Frenchman born in 1509, who moved to Switzerland in 1533 to avoid persecution. France has had a long history of persecution of Protestants, but freedom of worship was granted after the French Revolution. Differences in religion are not as important today. Most Protestants live in Paris, Alsace, the Massif Central, and on the western side of the country.

The fastest-growing religion in France today is Islam, with many Muslims immigrating to France from North Africa. Most of them are not fanatical about their religion and lead a Westernized lifestyle. Fundamentalism (a strict adherence to basic religious principles) is on the rise, however, and French authorities are closely watching its development.

Jews have lived in France for centuries, and French Jews form the largest Jewish community in Western Europe. They live primarily in Paris, Marseille, and in the Alsace region.

Below: **The Jewish quarter of Paris.**

Language and Literature

French is a Romance language and shares its roots with Italian, Spanish, Portuguese, and Romanian. It is derived from the Latin spoken by the Romans who conquered Gaul in 52 B.C. Prior to the Roman invasion, the people spoke Celtic languages. Today, only some people in Brittany still know Celtic.

The French language is characterized by flowing intonations and a more complex grammatical structure than English. The guardian of the language is the Académie Française. Founded in 1635 by Cardinal de Richelieu, one of the greatest prime ministers in French history, the Académie is made up of forty members called "immortals." They are chosen for life from the country's leading writers, scientists, lawyers, and military leaders. The Académie meets once a week to discuss ways to preserve the purity of the French language and to work toward making it the most glorious language in the world. Their main task is to write and edit the Dictionary of the French Academy. Despite their valiant efforts, other languages have influenced French, especially English. Words such as weekend, marketing, business, jogging, stress, and interview have all made it into everyday French conversations as well into written

LA FRANCOPHONIE

Because France was once a strong colonial power, many countries in Africa and Indochina still use French as an official language. Since 1986, French-speaking countries have come together in a grouping called La Francophonie (lah fran-ko-fo-NEE) to discuss world problems. This group of countries makes up 18 percent of the world economy and accounts for more than $100 billion in trade annually. About 250 million people speak French worldwide.

Left: Twentieth-century French literature includes writers such as Albert Camus, François Mauriac, and Jean Paul Sartre.

Far left: Victor Hugo (1802–1885) was an important writer of the nineteenth century. His writings integrated political and social commentary into stories of his times. Both *Les Misérables* and *The Hunchback of Notre Dame* have been translated into several languages.

Left: Aurore Dudevant (1804–1876), a nineteenth century writer, used the pen name "George Sand."

French. Many more words, however, have made their way from French into English. Some English words borrowed from French are: royal, chic, nouveau riche, gourmet, rendezvous, and cuisine.

Literature

The first great writer in France was François Rabelais, a Renaissance man. His *Gargantua* and *Pantagruel* have been translated into several languages and are still widely read today. *Gargantua* tells the story of a giant baby who ate enormous amounts of food. The English adjective "gargantuan," meaning a huge quantity, is derived from the name of the baby, Gargantua.

During the reign of Louis XIV, playwrights were popular, and Jean-Baptiste Molière, Pierre Corneille, and Jean Racine became famous. Molière wrote comedies; Corneille and Racine wrote tragedies.

In more recent times, French writers such as Victor Hugo, Alexandre Dumas (*The Three Musketeers*), Marcel Proust (*Remembrance of Things Past*), Jean Paul Sartre (*Human Being and Nothingness*), and Albert Camus (*The Alien*) have brought new ideas to the French literary scene.

Women writers, previously overshadowed by men, are now gaining recognition. Among contemporary women writers, Simone de Beauvoir stands out for her definitive feminist work, *The Second Sex*. Marguerite Duras, Marguerite Yourcenar, Françoise Sagan, and Hèléne Cixous are other women whose writings have earned them great critical acclaim.

TROUBADOURS

Troubadours were the first to use words to entertain others. Starting in the twelfth century, these traveling storytellers moved from one town square to another, narrating beautiful stories of love and adventure.
French literature was born in the Middle Ages when the epic stories were first recorded in manuscript form. *The Romance of the Rose* and *The Song of Roland* were well known.

Arts

Painting

The first paintings in France are more than fifteen thousand years old — wall paintings in the caves of Lascaux. During the Middle Ages, manuscript illumination flourished. The first real school of French painting emerged in the baroque period (late sixteenth to eighteenth centuries). Nicolas Poussin and Claude Lorrain painted landscapes, while Georges de la Tour and the Le Nain brothers observed family life in intimate detail. In the eighteenth century, Jacques Louis David was named official state painter by Napoleon. He generally produced vast paintings. The nineteenth century impressionist period was followed by postimpressionism, led by Paul Cézanne and Vincent van Gogh,

as well as Henri de Toulouse-Lautrec, who painted music-hall scenes. Two different styles emerged in the early twentieth century: Fauvism, which was characterized by the use of strong colors; and cubism, painting with geometric shapes. Next came the dadaists, who reacted to the negativity of World War I by challenging the concept of art and using objects in unexpected ways. Marcel "Dada" Duchamp exhibited various objects, including a urinal he titled *Fountain* and signed.

Top: **A painting by Édouard Manet, titled** *Argentueil*, **1874. Manet is considered the first painter of the Modern era and was the forerunner of the impressionists.**

Above: **The Louvre in Paris is a well-known art museum.**

Music and Film

The early nineteenth century witnessed the musical genius of Hector Berlioz and Frédéric Chopin. The inventor of modern orchestration, Berlioz's works sparked a musical rebirth in France. Although Polish by birth, Chopin lived in Paris and influenced later French composers. His music is marked by his unique sense of lyricism and unparalleled melodic genius. Claude Debussy and Maurice Ravel represented Impressionism in music. Their contemporaries include Georges Bizet and Camille Saint-Saëns.

Frenchmen Louis and Auguste Lumiere share credit with American Thomas Edison for the invention of cinema in the late nineteenth century. The Lumiere brothers manufactured a portable camera projector called the Cinématographe, based on Edison's inventions. French films today are renowned for their artistic content and strong emphasis on individuals and moods.

IMPRESSIONISM

Impressionism is the most famous French school of painting. Led by Claude Monet, impressionists tried to capture the shimmering quality of light in their paintings. Although impressionism lasted only a few years in the late nineteenth century, it left an enormous legacy of paintings, which now grace the walls of museums all over the world.
(*A Closer Look, page 58*)

Left: The most famous and oldest film festival in France is in Cannes. This festival has launched the careers of several leading actors including French actor Brigitte Bardot. Held yearly since 1946 in this small resort town, the festival showcases some of the best films produced in the world.

31

Architecture

Emerging from the Dark Ages in the eleventh century, France witnessed a blossoming of architecture. The Romanesque style, with thick walls, rounded arches, and heavy vaults, was based on buildings common in Roman times. The first distinctly French architecture was the Gothic style. Originating in the twelfth century in northern France, it used pointed arches and flying buttresses as supports, which allowed for taller buildings with larger windows.

During the Renaissance, buildings were largely based on the Italian model, stressing harmony and symmetry. The baroque style that followed used the same style of building, but introduced elaborate gardens with fountains, hedges, and clipped trees. The Versailles Palace, built by Louis XIV, is a famous example.

Rural architecture is the product of local materials and varies with climate and topography. Roofs in the north are steeply sloped and covered with flat tiles to allow rain water to run off easily. In the south, where there are strong winds, roofs are broad and covered with rounded tiles. French farmhouses fall into three categories: the *maison bloc* (may-zohn BLOC), where house and outbuildings share the same roof; the high house, with living quarters upstairs and livestock or wine cellars below; and courtyard farmsteads where the buildings are set around a central court.

Above: **The Cathedral of Notre Dame in Paris is one of the most famous Gothic structures. Its construction went on for almost two hundred years! Along with pointed arches and flying buttresses, the Gothic style is characterized by delicate spires and beautiful stained glass.**

Left: A Breton woman makes lace. Brittany has remained relatively isolated from the rest of France through the centuries. As a result, its language, Breton, and some of its unique traditions have been preserved. One such tradition is making lace, which is then used to make intricate *coiffes* (KWAF), the headdress that forms part of the traditional Breton costume.

CAN YOU DO THE CANCAN?

The French cancan is the most well-known form of French dancing. Under their wide skirts, cancan dancers wear bloomers and layers of petticoats, which they show off while kicking their legs in the air. Dating from the 1830s, French cancan is a highly energetic dance with an infectious rhythm. Classical and modern ballet are also very popular in France. In fact, the vocabulary and techniques of ballet were developed by Marius Petitpas at the beginning of this century. Some of his best-known choreographies are *Sleeping Beauty* and *The Nutcracker*.

Traditional Crafts

Although most traditional forms of arts and crafts are slowly disappearing, lace-making in Brittany is actually experiencing a revival, along with the Breton culture. Embroidery on aprons is also a specialty of the region. In Betschdorf, Alsace, pottery skills are passed down from generation to generation. Men typically glaze the pots in a characteristic blue-gray color, while the women decorate them in cobalt blue. Limoges is well known for its porcelain and glassware.

Leisure and Festivals

Outdoor Fun

Most French city-dwellers like to go to the countryside to take a break. On weekends or for long vacations, many escape to their second homes in the countryside. (The French have the highest rate of second home ownership in Europe.) Breathing in the fresh air, walking to the village café for a drink, or puttering about in the garden is enough to recharge most people. One very popular activity is hiking. Adults and children enjoy long walks in the woods, discovering the local flora and fauna. They pick wild berries and mushrooms when they are in season, and cook and serve the mushrooms for dinner.

Above: **Biking through the countryside on a beautiful summer day is a popular activity.**

In general, French families like to spend their free time together. In the spring and summer, they go to outdoor parks to ride bicycles, stroll, or watch puppet shows. In big cities, museums, zoos, and aquariums are crowded with young families.

On weekends, many Parisian youngsters congregate at the Trocadéro beneath the Eiffel Tower or at the Arch of La Défense to meet with friends or to show off their roller-skating prowess. The more adventurous ones perform amazing tricks.

Boules

Boules is a kind of bowling game played with two large metal balls and a smaller one called *cochonnet* (ko-cho-NAY). The game is very popular among older men, and every park or village square has a little boules arena made of packed earth. Any number of players can take part, and the aim of the game is to throw a ball close to the cochonnet. Knocking an opponent's ball is allowed, and the winner is the one whose ball lands closest to the cochonnet.

Theme Parks

The two most popular theme parks in France are Parc Astérix, north of Paris, and Euro Disney in Marne-la-Vallée. Euro Disney attracts visitors from throughout Europe. Part of the park, Discoveryland, is based on the novels of Jules Verne.

ASTERIX THE GAUL

This well-loved comic-strip has inspired a theme park, Parc Astérix. The adventures of Asterix and Obelix are based on life in the time of the Gauls, a Celtic tribe conquered by the Romans in the first century.
(A Closer Look, page 44)

Left: Pétanque (pay-TAHNK)**, very popular in the south of France, is played along the same principles as boules and with the same number of balls, except the balls are thrown in the air rather than rolled on the ground.**

35

Above: **A skiing lesson in the Alps. Many people take a couple of weeks off in the winter and go skiing.**

Soccer

Soccer is probably the most popular sport in France. Called football, or *le foot*, it is played at all levels and by people of all ages. Each city has its own team, and the best ones take part in the French championship. Professional matches are played on weekends and attract huge crowds. In 1998, France played host to the World Cup for soccer. The best teams in the world competed for a chance to take home the prestigious trophy. It was France itself, however, that scored a stunning victory in the finals against Brazil and won the World Cup for the very first time in the history of the competition.

In a display of French humor, the mascot of the games was a cockerel called Footix. The cockerel is the emblem of France, and the name Footix combines both football and the Gallic spirit of Asterix.

Cycling and Other Sports

Although team sports attract the most spectators, the French prefer individual sports, such as tennis, cycling, horseback riding, and sailing. The two most popular sporting events in the summer are the Roland Garros tennis tournament and the cycling Tour de France. Not only do these events draw huge crowds, but they also attract the best athletes in the world to compete.

TOUR DE FRANCE

For three weeks, the best cyclists in the world race in the Tour de France.

(*A Closer Look,* page 70)

Presents and Crowns

Christmas and Easter Sunday are important family occasions. The whole family usually gets together at the grandparents' house for a sumptuous meal. January 6, Twelfth Night in the Christian calendar, is an important day for all children. It is called the festival of kings. A large pastry, called a *galette* (gah-LET), has a bean or other surprise inside. The child who finds it in his or her piece gets to be king or queen of the day and wear a paper crown. He or she picks a partner, and for the rest of the day, the king and queen are treated with mock deference.

Carnival

Carnival is one last occasion to have fun before Lent (the season of fasting and abstinence for Catholics). Many towns hold parades with floats and revelers dressed in costumes and masks. The festivities end with the Carnival ball and a fireworks display. The most exuberant Carnival takes place in Nice, where twelve days are devoted to feasting and dancing. The celebrations culminate in the spectacular Battle of the Flowers, a parade of floats and people dressed with flowers.

Below: **Captain Hook and his crew have joined this Carnival parade in Nice!**

Bastille Day

July 14, generally regarded as the start of the French Revolution, marks the day the Paris mob stormed the Bastille prison. This day is commemorated as France's national day. The French flag, or tricolor, adorns government offices and public places. Parades are organized in every town, and the mayor makes a speech in the town square. In Paris, the president and other dignitaries watch a military parade featuring tanks, armored vehicles, helicopters, and Mirage fighter jets. In the evening, the skies are lit up with a magnificent display of fireworks. The medieval town of Carcassonne in the south of France puts on a splendid sound and light performance.

Harvest Festivals

The most important harvest festivals are those marking the *vendanges* (vahn-DAHNJE), the harvesting of wine grapes in September. Members of wine societies, in ceremonial costumes, taste the wines and make speeches. *Les Trois Glorieuses* (lay trwa glo-REEUZ) are three days devoted to wine in Burgundy. On the third Saturday of November, a large banquet brings together the best wine-tasters of the country. On Sunday, a charity auction of wine is the highlight of the festival. The prices are the benchmark for the entire batch of wine. Finally, on Monday, the festival ends with a party where the wine growers of the region bring their best bottles of wine to enjoy.

Saint Torpes

La Bravade (lah bra-VAD) honors Saint Torpes, the patron saint of Saint-Tropez. Saint Torpes was a Roman soldier who was martyred for being a Christian by Emperor Nero. Every year in May, an effigy of the saint is carried through the town to the accompaniment of musket fire. The carriers are dressed in red and hold a musket.

Avignon Festival

France's largest festival, the Avignon Festival, was founded in 1947 by the well-known actors Gérard Philipe and Jean Vilar. From mid-July to mid-August, this southern town plays host to ballet and drama performances as well as classical concerts. Street theater and music from folk to jazz are also part of the festival.

Above: **Bastille Day. The Eiffel Tower in Paris is lit up with a spectacular display of fireworks in blue, white, and red, France's national colors.**

BUILDER OF MONUMENTS

The Eiffel Tower was designed by Gustave Eiffel for the 1889 International Exhibition in Paris. People considered it an eyesore and it was almost torn down afterward, but has since become a well-loved landmark in Paris.
(A Closer Look, page 46)

Brittany Festivals

Brittany has many festivals celebrating the region's Celtic roots. Celts from Cornwall and Wales fled to the region in the fifth and sixth centuries. Their influence on the language, customs, and religion has remained strong. Celts have been coming to Quimper in July every year since 1923 to witness a revival of Celtic culture in the Festival de Cornouaille. Bretons, as people in Brittany are called, dress in the traditional clothes of clogs and lace coiffes, special hats made of lace. Bagpipers accompany traditional dances. Men have wrestling matches and women show off their embroidery skills.

Another festival peculiar to Brittany is the religious *pardon* (pahr-DOHN), which is celebrated on a saint's day to grant pardon for the people's sins of the past year. In fact, there are several pardons during the year. Some pardons attract many thousands of pilgrims. The rector blesses motorbikes at the Biker's Pardon in Morbihan every August 15. On the last Sunday of July, an Islamic-Christian pilgrimage takes place at Vieux Marché. Catholic masses as well as Muslim prayers are said.

Above: **A parade for the Festival de Cornouaille in Quimper, Brittany. Everyone dresses up in traditional Breton clothes. Girls and women wear hats made of lace, while boys and men wear baggy cotton trousers.**

Food

Each region in France has its food specialties, based on the produce available. In general, the cuisine of the north uses butter and dairy products, while southern dishes contain olive oil, tomatoes, and herbs. Along the coast, seafood is plentiful. Oysters are a favorite on the Atlantic coast. They are eaten raw or broiled and served with a cream sauce. The traditional seafood platter includes oysters, clams, mussels, crawfish, crabs, shrimps, and periwinkles. They are boiled and eaten with lemons and a shallot and vinegar sauce. Along the Mediterranean, seafood is usually cooked in a *bouillabaisse* (boo-yah-BES), a rich stew of fish, tomatoes, wine, olive oil, and saffron.

France's favorite food has to be bread, especially the long, thin loaf called *baguette* (ba-GET). When eaten as a sandwich, it is split in two lengthwise and filled with butter, cheese, ham, paté, or salami. Children love *tartines* (tar-TEEN), sliced bread spread with butter, jam, honey, or soft cheese.

American-style fast foods have now invaded France, and many young people prefer to have a burger and fries rather than a traditional French meal. North African kebabs are also appearing in many of the larger towns.

Above: **Baking bread. The French make delicious breads, including baguettes, croissants, and brioche, a soft bread made with flour, yeast, butter, milk, and eggs. Bread is so important that by law every village must have at least one shop making or selling bread daily.**

Meal Times

The day begins with bread, either a croissant or a tartine for everyone in the family. It is all washed down with milk or hot chocolate for young children and coffee for adults and teenagers. Served in a bowl-shaped cup, *café au lait* (ka-fay oh LAY) is coffee with a generous dose of milk. Some families also eat yogurt or fresh, white cheese. Another popular snack for children after they get home from school is *pain au chocolat* (pehn o sho-ko-LAH), a flaky pastry baked with a bar of chocolate in the middle.

Lunch used to be the main meal of the day, but many families now eat a very light lunch because of work and school commitments. The usual dishes are sandwiches, salads, quiche, or pasta. On Sundays, families sit down together for a more

GOURMET FOOD AND FINE WINE

French foods and wines are world famous. Normandy and Brittany produce the best dairy products and apples in the country, while the Loire Valley and Champagne are well-known wine regions. Burgundy and Franche-Comté are known for both wine and cheese.

(*A Closer Look, page 56*)

substantial lunch consisting of salad, soup, a casserole or roast, and dessert. Favorite dishes are steak with fries or roast chicken with vegetables.

The last meal of the day is dinner, eaten rather late between 7:00 and 9:30 p.m. Adults generally have three courses consisting of soup, ham, or salad, followed by a steak or lamb stew, and a dessert or cheese and fruit. They usually drink wine with the meal and sometimes have strong coffee afterward. Children, however, may skip the main course and eat soup with bread or a slice of cheese.

Above: **For lunch, the café or** *brasserie* **(brass-REE) is a popular choice. Tables are small and arranged close together, and most customers prefer to sit outside on the sidewalk, where they can watch the world go by.**

A CLOSER LOOK AT FRANCE

This section highlights the people, places, ideas, and festivals that are close to the French heart. Among the most celebrated women in France are Joan of Arc, who saved the country from English invasion, and the scientist Marie Curie, the only person to have won the Nobel Prize twice. The Sun King and the comic-book character Asterix are well loved because they display characteristics that are admired by the French people: the glorification of France and an indomitable spirit against bullies.

Below: **An outdoor market in Normandy with local specialties for sale.**

The French people are justly proud of their fine wines, great food, and wonderful perfumes. The guillotine, however, is a French invention that many might prefer the world forget!

Paris is the most important city in France. It exudes grandeur and glamor, attracting people from around the world, including many artists. It has been central to new movements in art, such as impressionism. In contrast, the Camargue region in the southwest is wild and beautiful. Mont-Saint-Michel, on the northern coast, is registered as a natural and cultural monument, but faces new environmental challenges.

Opposite: **This whimsical sculpture is part of a group of brightly colored, moving sculptures in the Stravinsky fountain in Paris. Each sculpture represents one of the compositions of musician Igor Stravinsky.**

Asterix the Gaul

Parc Astérix

Parc Astérix, which lies just north of Paris, is France's answer to Disneyland. It is built to resemble a fortified Gallic village and Roman encampment. It has its own customs controls, currency, FM radio station, and security staff wearing plastic winged helmets. The park's old-fashioned merry-go-rounds and high-speed thrill rides are all based on the adventures of comic-strip character Asterix.

Asterix the Gaul was born in 1959, first as a comic-strip hero in a magazine, then in a 48-page comic book. His parents were writer René Goscinny and artist Alberto Uderzo. In the stories, Asterix lives in a small village in Gaul that is valiantly fighting the Roman Empire. His best friend is Obelix, a fat menhir maker, or maker of tall, stone monuments, who likes to hit Roman legionnaires and eat roasted wild boar. Asterix, Obelix, and the dog Dogmatix enjoy numerous adventures spread over thirty books. Asterix travels to other nations, rescue damsels in distress, and even meets Cleopatra, in addition to knocking out thousands of Roman soldiers. He gets his superhuman strength from a magic potion brewed by the village druid (medicine man), Magigimmix. Even the village elder, Arthritix, is able to box and kick his way through

Above: Asterix in Belgium, one of many titles. Asterix is a beloved character because he represents the indomitable Gallic spirit fighting against oppression. Modern French people descend from the Gauls, and they admire the tenacity of the underdog represented by Asterix and his village.

Left: **Gaul warriors. The most famous Gaul was Vercingetorix, who managed to defeat the Roman army in 52 B.C. His success, however, was short-lived because he was captured the following year by Julius Caesar in the siege of a town in Burgundy. Vercingetorix was taken to Rome as a prisoner and was ritually strangled six years later. He is a romantic figure for the French people because he died young in a fight against the Roman invasion.**

a Roman squadron when he takes the potion. Punctuating their punches with exclamations such as "By Toutatis" (the Celtic god of war) or "By Belenus" (the god of light), the fearless Gauls can demolish an entire army of Roman soldiers in no time at all.

Who Were the Gauls?

The Gauls were Celts who migrated to France in about 1500 B.C. They shared a common stock with the people of the British Isles and generally had dark hair and dark eyes. Ancient Gaul had an urbanized society with well-laid-out streets, specialized areas for craftspeople, and public buildings. Gauls were strongly opposed to dictators, and all decisions were made by a public assembly. Some settlements even had rules to ensure that no one person could have absolute power. Celtic influence is still strong today in Normandy and Brittany.

Opposite: **Obelix leads the way! The Asterix comic books come alive in a reconstructed Gallic village and a Roman camp in Parc Astérix.**

Builder of Monuments

Gustave Eiffel

Born in Dijon in 1832, Gustave Eiffel was formally trained as a chemist, but he started his professional life in an engineering firm. Eiffel proved to be such a good engineer that he was put in charge of building the Bordeaux Bridge in 1858. The first bridge of its kind, it established Eiffel as the foremost builder of bridges, and he was soon able to set up his own building company. He went on to build bridges all over the world, from Peru to the Philippines. A totally different monument, however, would bring Eiffel eternal renown: the Eiffel Tower in Paris. Denounced by many artists at

the time as a monstrosity, the Eiffel Tower today is the most recognizable landmark of France. Eiffel built the tower as a doorway for the 1889 International Exhibition in Paris. It took two years to build and cost nearly eight million francs. Soaring to a height of 989 feet (301 m), the tower required two million rivets to hold it in place. It was assembled, inch by inch, on the very spot where it still stands today. When the Eiffel Tower was inaugurated on March 31, 1889, it was greeted as a triumph by

Top: **Gustave Eiffel.**

Above: **The Eiffel Tower is a marvel of lightness. If you look at it from any angle, you will always be able to see the sky through it. On a clear day, the view from the top extends over 50 miles (80 km).**

the Parisian public. In the first six months, almost two million visitors climbed the tower.

According to initial plans, the Eiffel Tower was to be dismantled when the Exhibition ended. Many people saw it as an eyesore on the Paris landscape. Eiffel, however, won a reprieve for his project by demonstrating its value as an antenna for a new invention, the radio. Today, the Eiffel Tower houses radio, television, and telecommunications transmitters.

Gustave Eiffel was a man of vision and innovation, a true scientist. After building two of the most well-known landmarks in the world, he devoted his later years to the study of aerodynamics. Even at the age of eighty-eight, he wrote a treatise on propellers. Eiffel died in 1924, when he was ninety-two years old.

THE STATUE OF LIBERTY

The man who built the Eiffel Tower was also behind one of the great landmarks of America, the Statue of Liberty. The metal skeleton for the statue was designed and built by Gustave Eiffel in Paris. The statue itself was made in France and first displayed in Paris. It was then disassembled and sent by ship to the United States, where it was unveiled in New York Harbor in 1886.

Left: A smaller Statue of Liberty stands on an islet in the middle of the Seine river in Paris. It faces west toward the original Statue of Liberty across the ocean.

The City of Lights

An Ancient Settlement

Paris, the capital of France, takes its name from the Parisii, a Celtic tribe that settled on an island in the middle of the Seine River in the third century B.C. In 53 B.C., the Romans conquered the village and named it *Lutetia Parisiorum*. Soon, Lutetia became a center for trade, which it still is today. The city took its present name "Paris" in the eighth century.

Modern Paris was built in the second half of the nineteenth century by Baron Haussmann, the prefect (chief city official) of the Seine. Many old buildings were razed to make way for well-laid-out streets that followed a geometric grid. Modern buildings of glass and iron were erected, and Paris got a new water supply and sewage systems. As gas lighting became available, tourists from everywhere flocked to see the renovated Paris, the City of Lights.

One of the wonders of Haussmann's street network is the star-shaped Place de l'Étoile. Twelve grand avenues, including the splendid Champs Elysées, radiate outward from the Arc de

Below: **A view of Paris from the Notre Dame Cathedral. The Eiffel Tower is visible in the distance. The strange statue on the left is known as a gargoyle. It is on the corner of the cathedral building and spouts rainwater from its mouth.**

Triomphe like spokes from the hub of a wheel. The Arc itself is one of the highlights of Paris. It was built from 1806 to 1836, following Napoleon's victory at the Battle of Austerlitz.

A Vibrant City

The Seine River divides Paris into the Left Bank and the Right Bank. The Left Bank is one of the most vibrant districts of Paris. It is associated with poets, philosophers, and artists. The Latin Quarter is its most ancient area, populated since Roman times. It takes its name from the Latin-speaking students of the Sorbonne, the first university in France. From its modest origins, with only sixteen poor students, the Sorbonne has now become the University of Paris and has been split into thirteen separate universities. People still refer to it, however, as the Sorbonne. The name has much prestige.

Paris is also well known for its fashionable shops, entertainment, and outdoor cafés, where people can watch the world go by. The French cancan was invented at the Moulin Rouge, one of the most famous cabarets in Paris.

Above: **Eating at cafés and outdoor restaurants is an important part of French life, and people may linger for many hours.**

Deadly Invention

The guillotine was invented by Doctor Joseph Ignace Guillotin (1738–1814) as a more "humane and private" form of capital punishment. Prior to its adoption in 1792, executions were public events where criminals were tortured to death in front of a large crowd. Only upper-class criminals were executed swiftly and in private. Dr. Guillotin worked on a device that would make death swift and painless, thus preserving the dignity of the criminal. In fact, Dr. Guillotin was against the execution of criminals and invented the guillotine as a step toward the abolition of the death penalty. It is ironic that his invention today is associated with the very notion of punishment.

Above: **The guillotine.**

The guillotine is a structure with a sharp blade that drops from a height of 88 inches (223 centimeters) to cut off the head of a condemned person in a swift and effective movement. The blade itself is slanted at a 45-degree angle and weighs about 90 pounds (41 kilograms). An actual beheading takes less than a second.

The guillotine gained prominence during the French Revolution. After the storming of the Bastille in 1789, the new National Assembly decreed that, in the spirit of equality, the guillotine was to be used for all beheadings. The first such execution took place in April 1792. Ironically, King Louis XVI, the one who had approved Dr. Guillotin's device in the first place, was guillotined in January 1793. In another twist of fate, Robespierre, one of the leaders of the Revolution, also fell to the guillotine. He went from ordering the executions of the aristocrats, and all those who were opposed to the new regime, to being a victim of the guillotine when he was beheaded in 1794.

The period after the King's death was a frightful time when thousands of people of all ages were killed, sometimes for no reason. The guillotine became the symbol of the Reign of Terror, as this period was called. During the last six weeks of the Reign of Terror, nearly fourteen hundred people were guillotined in Paris alone. In the hands of the ruling factions, the guillotine was an instrument of extermination, and executions were a public celebration.

The last execution by guillotine took place in Marseille in 1977 when the murderer Hamida Djandoubi was beheaded. France has since abolished capital punishment.

Opposite: **Marie Antoinette, queen of France at the time of the Revolution, was executed by guillotine in 1793.**

51

Famous French Scientists

France has often been at the forefront of scientific discovery, inventing medical machines and creating drugs that have saved millions of lives. It was a French team that isolated the HIV virus, and the Pasteur Institute in Paris is working hard to find a cure for AIDS. Marie Curie and Louis Pasteur were two of the most prominent scientists in French history.

Marie Curie

Marie Curie was born in Poland in 1867. In 1891, she went to Paris to study physics and mathematics. She married Pierre Curie in 1895, and the couple started to research the radioactive properties of uranium. At a time when many women were denied even a basic education, Marie threw herself wholeheartedly into her research. While Pierre observed the properties of radiation, she purified the radioactive elements. She discovered polonium and

Left: **Marie and Pierre Curie worked together on radiation research. Marie Curie justly deserves to be known as one of the foremost French women scientists. She studied radioactivity. In fact, the word "radioactive" was coined by Marie. For her outstanding achievements, Marie Curie (together with Pierre) was honored with the Nobel Prize in 1903. She received a second Nobel Prize in 1911 and is the only person ever to receive the award twice.**

Left: **Louis Pasteur's research on germs has been invaluable in the field of medicine. One of his greatest contributions was the process of immunization. He discovered that when people are injected with weakened forms of certain germs, they develop an immunity to those germs and will not get the disease. This discovery has saved, and will continue to save, billions of lives. Pasteur developed vaccines against chicken pox, cholera, anthrax, and swine fever.**

radium, two very important minerals. When Pierre died in 1906, Marie took up his position at the Sorbonne University. She was the first woman to be appointed professor there. Her research would have immense medical value to all humankind because radioactivity became the starting point for cancer treatment. Ironically, in 1934, Marie Curie died of leukemia (a form of cancer) due to years of exposure to high levels of radiation.

Louis Pasteur

Louis Pasteur is best known for the technique of pasteurization. This process uses heat to destroy harmful microorganisms present in perishable food products, such as milk and beer, and prevents food from spoiling. Pasteurization would not have been invented, however, without Pasteur's prior research on germs. His discovery that most infectious diseases are caused by germs is one of the most important in medical history. Because of this new knowledge, doctors and hospitals became conscious of how diseases are spread and took steps to prevent contamination.

The Pasteur Institute opened in 1888 as a research center for infectious diseases, and Louis Pasteur devoted the last years of his life to the Institute. He died in 1895.

STOPPING RABIES

Pasteur's most important vaccine was against rabies. Before 1885, rabies was rampant, and people bitten by rabid dogs would die in horrific pain. Pasteur's vaccine enabled veterinarians to immunize dogs against rabies. The vaccine was also developed into a cure for people bitten by rabid dogs.

The Four Corners of the World

A Former Empire

In the nineteenth century, France built an impressive colonial empire spanning parts of Africa, Indochina in Southeast Asia, and numerous islands in the Pacific and Indian oceans and in the Caribbean. Its holdings in North America included Louisiana and Quebec. Today, all that remains of this empire is a handful of small territories in various corners of the world. These territories are divided into overseas departments (which go by the acronym DOM) and overseas territories (TOM).

Overseas departments function just like any other department in France. For all intents and purposes, DOM are considered an integral part of France. The inhabitants of

Above: **Vietnam was colonized by the French, along with Cambodia and Laos. Some of the older, educated Vietnamese still speak French and wear French-style hats.**

Left: **A woman selling fruit and flowers in French Polynesia. The cluster of islands of French Polynesia is a territory of France.**

Martinique and Guadeloupe in the Caribbean, French Guyana in South America, and Reunion in the Indian Ocean make up 2.5 percent of the total French population. They are considered French citizens and can move freely between their homeland and France. They take part in national, provincial, and European Union elections, and the men are called up for military service.

Overseas territories include New Caledonia, French Polynesia, Wallis and Futuna islands in the Pacific, and the French Southern and Antarctic Holdings in Antarctica. Mayotte in the Indian Ocean and Saint Pierre and Miquelon off eastern Canada are called territorial collectivities. Inhabitants of TOM have the same rights as French citizens and elect their representatives to the National Assembly in Paris, but overseas territories also have a certain amount of self-government. They are free to set their own internal policies, although France still dictates foreign policy and finance. Pro-independence elements in the TOM do not see themselves as any better than the DOM. In fact, they are tied to French national policies in many spheres, yet they do not receive the same benefits as French departments.

The economies of the overseas departments and territories are closely tied to the French economy. They trade with each other and with France. New Caledonia exports a variety of zucchini to Japan. All DOM-TOM are highly dependent on agriculture but are not self-sufficient in any product. Their economies and infrastructure are still in the early stages of development. The DOM-TOM receive massive aid from France. This aid, however, comes with strings attached, as in the case of French Polynesia, where the French government has conducted nuclear tests.

Below: Haiti was also a French colony in the eighteenth century. Vast plantations and a thriving slave trade made Haiti, or St. Domingue as it was then called, the richest colony in the French Empire. The French language is still an official language of Haiti, along with Creole, but only the educated upper and middle classes use it.

Francophonie

Although most of the former colonies are now independent, they are all bound by a common language and heritage, called La Francophonie. The Cambodian, the Senegalese, and the Quebecker can all understand and relate to each other through a shared colonial history. Unlike the British Commonwealth, which is more of a political and economic entity, this group is more interested in its cultural, historical, and linguistic heritage. However, French President Jacques Chirac would like to see the grouping grow into something similar to the Commonwealth, with more emphasis on trade and economy, yet retain its cultural functions.

Gourmet Food and Fine Wines

A Love of Good Food

French food and wines are the most well known in the world. The French are passionate about their food and extremely knowledgeable when it comes to specialities of different regions. For instance, there are more than three hundred and fifty different varieties of cheeses. Some are hard, some soft; some are flavored with herbs, nuts, or peppercorns. The world's favorite French cheese is Camembert, which originated in the small town of Camembert in Normandy. Cow's milk curd is left to set for a day, and then is salted and sprayed with a bacterium, forming the white bloom on the surface of the cheese and encouraging the cheese to ripen. As the Camembert gets older, the center turns soft and flavorful.

Other famous French gourmet foods are black truffles and *foie gras* (fwa GRAH) from Périgord in the southwest. Foie gras is the fattened liver of goose or duck. The birds are allowed to wander and feed outdoors until they reach a certain size. Then they are

TRUFFLES

Called "black diamonds," black truffles are one of the most famous and expensive luxury foods in France. The warty fungus grows underground in the roots of oak and hazelnut trees and is harvested in winter by specially-trained sniffing dogs and pigs.

Below: A shop selling cheeses. Made from cow's, goat's, or ewe's milk, French cheeses range from hard and dry mountain cheese to soft and runny, white Camembert.

fed with corn to fatten up their livers. After the animals have been slaughtered, the livers are kept in goose or duck fat before cooking. Its manufacturing process is cruel, but foie gras is a delicacy that has been enjoyed since antiquity and is still one of the most sought-after foods in the world.

Fine Wines

For several centuries, France has enjoyed a reputation for producing the best wines in the world. Red and white wines vary greatly from region to region. The quality of a wine depends very much on the soil in which the grape vines are planted and the weather during the growing season. The wine is produced from grapes through the process of fermentation. Champagne and Cognac are two of the most famous wines.

Champagne, the finest sparkling wine in the world, is produced in the region of Champagne in northern France. To make Champagne, three different wines are mixed together and put into bottles with a little yeast. The yeast causes the wines to ferment one more time, resulting in fine bubbles. It is a very slow process, and the bottles have to remain on their sides for at least fifteen months. The longer the fermentation, the better the Champagne.

Above: **Grapes are harvested in the late summer or fall every year. They are then crushed and left to ferment. Good years for wine occur when summer comes early and the vines are harvested before September. Grapes used to make wine are different varieties from those eaten.**

Impressionism

The word *impressionist* was first used mockingly by a journalist to describe a painting by Claude Monet in 1874 entitled *Impression: Sunrise*. Many artists recognized their style in the word "impressionism" and continued to use the term. Impressionist painters are highly respected today for their talent and innovative genius.

    Most impressionist works of art were painted between 1867 and 1886. The impressionist movement was touched off by painter Édouard Manet's *Luncheon on the Grass,* which was exhibited in 1863. Manet himself was not an impressionist, but his work influenced a group of painters who rejected the conventional techniques and concepts of painting. This group, consisting of Claude Monet, Pierre Auguste Renoir, Camille Pissarro, Alfred Sisley, Berthe Morisot, Armand Guillaumin, and Frédéric Bazille, did not see a painting as a fixed record of an object or landscape. Instead, Impressionist painters tried to capture a moment in time because objects and landscapes look different at different times of the day. They aimed to reproduce

Above: Vincent van Gogh, self-portrait.

Left: Luncheon on the Grass by Édouard Manet. Manet broke away from the art conventions of his time, and this painting shocked many when it was first exhibited.

immediate visual impressions rather than paint something as it would normally look. The main characteristic of impressionism was an attempt to record the transient effects of light and color. Thus, painters would paint different versions of the same subject, but in different lights. Claude Monet, especially, did not tire of painting the same scenes over and over again at different times of the day. His series of paintings of Rouen Cathedral exemplifies the impressionist philosophy very well.

Since the official Salon of the French Academy consistently rejected their works, the impressionists held their own exhibitions. The first show took place in 1874. Altogether, there were eight shows until 1886. The group dissolved afterward because the members wanted to pursue their own interests in painting techniques and subject matter.

Impressionism lasted only twenty years, but it left a lasting legacy in the history of art. Today, impressionist paintings are exhibited in museums all over the world, including the United States, and are highly prized by art collectors. Postimpressionist artists, such as Vincent van Gogh, Edgar Degas, and Paul Gauguin, were influenced by the impressionist movement and produced a body of work that represents the best in modern art.

Maid of Orléans

Joan of Arc, also called the Maid of Orléans, was born on January 6, 1412, in the village of Domrémy in eastern France. Like most children of her time, she did not go to school but learned to sew and spin from her mother. She was very pious and often went to church.

At the time of Joan's birth, the Hundred Years' War (1337–1453) between the French and the English was still raging. The village of Domrémy actually came under the rule of an ally of the English, the Duke of Burgundy, but the villagers continued to be loyal to the French king, Charles VII. When Joan was thirteen, she became aware of voices in her head telling her to fight the English. At first she refused to listen, but by the time she was sixteen, she became convinced that her duty was to help the king. In March 1429, she presented herself to Charles VII and offered to lead his armies. As a test, Charles disguised himself as one of the royal attendants, but Joan recognized him immediately even though she had never laid eyes on him before.

After Joan proved her good faith, the king gave her some troops, and she went into battle. On May 8, 1429, she ended the siege of the town of Orléans and later captured the English forts in the area. Joan was not a trained soldier, but her spirit and conviction raised the morale of her troops, and they fought with great courage. The French army went from victory to victory, and Charles was crowned at Reims on July 17, only three months after Joan joined the battle.

Some of the king's followers resented the presence of Joan of Arc. During a failed assault on the town of Compiègne, in May 1429, she was taken prisoner by the Burgundian army and sold to the English. On the advice of people hostile to Joan, the French king left her to her fate. The English and Burgundians were determined to kill her, but they could not do so just because she had defeated them. So they turned her over to the religious court at Rouen to be tried as a witch. The proceedings were long and tortuous, but, throughout the two years of the trial, Joan never once betrayed her faith. She was burned at the stake in the market place at Rouen on May 30, 1431. She was only nineteen.

Today, Joan of Arc is a symbol of courage and perseverance, and is one of the most respected historical figures among French children.

Above: **Joan of Arc led the armies of French King Charles VII to repeated victories against the English. Although she suffered injuries in battles and was later burned at the stake, she never betrayed her faith or convictions. The city of Orléans celebrates her memory every year with a festival in April and May, when the liberation of the city is reenacted.**

Opposite: **Joan of Arc was burned at the stake as a witch in 1431. Twenty-five years later, a new trial took place in Paris that overturned the guilty verdict of the first trial, reinstating Joan's reputation and starting the process to make her a saint. In 1920, Joan of Arc became Saint Joan.**

Mont-Saint-Michel

Tidal Waves and an Island

Just off the coast of northern France, an isolated piece of granite rises out of the sea. This island stands at the mouth of the river Couesnon and lies on the border between Brittany and Normandy. It takes its name from the abbey that perches high on top of the island, Mont-Saint-Michel. It was once part of the French mainland, and the highest point in the forest of Scissy. In the year A.D. 709, a huge tidal wave engulfed the forest, turning the hillock into an island. It is now surrounded by large sand banks and becomes an island during high tides. Mont-Saint-Michel and its bay are registered on the UNESCO worldwide patrimony list as part of France's natural and cultural heritage.

Below: The abbey of Mont-Saint-Michel sits on the peak of the island. Its tower and spire reach far into the sky. The tides in the surrounding bay are very strong and act as a natural defense. Rising and falling with the movements of the moon, they can reach speeds of 18 miles (29 km) per hour in the spring.

The Abbey of Saint-Michel

Legend has it that, in the year of the tidal wave, the archangel Michael appeared three times before Saint Aubert, the bishop of Avranches, requesting that a shrine be built to him. An oratory was built in the eighth century, and in A.D. 966, twelve Benedictine monks founded the abbey dedicated to Saint Michael. It became a center of learning in the twelfth and thirteenth centuries. Pilgrims,

including large numbers of children, known as *miquelots* (mik-KE-loh) journeyed great distances to honor the cult of Saint Michael. After the French Revolution, the abbey became a political prison for seventy-three years. One of the reminders of this trying time is Gaultier's Leap, a terrace near the top of the church that was named after a prisoner who leaped to his death from there. Today, a small community of Benedictine monks still lives in the abbey.

Saving Mont-Saint-Michel

Mont-Saint-Michel lies only half a mile (0.8 km) from the mainland. At low tide, the sea retreats, leaving a large expanse of sand. Formerly, crossing the sand was the only way to reach the island. Today, a road links it to the mainland.

Unfortunately, the road has brought problems. Sand has been collecting in the bay, and now the island is cut off from the mainland only during high tides. Environmental experts and the inhabitants of Mont-Saint-Michel fear that the island will soon be permanently connected to the mainland as the seabed rises.

The French government has embarked on a seven-year project to protect the island. The road will be replaced by a bridge. Having a bridge that crosses the sea instead of a road that sits in it will allow sand to circulate naturally in the bay, greatly lessening the problem of silting. At a cost of nearly 1 billion dollars, the project hopes to maintain the island's maritime character.

A Nose for Perfumes

The perfume industry in France has flourished since King Louis XIV's reign. The Sun King and his courtiers did not take much care of their personal hygiene. Instead, they relied on perfumes to mask odors. Today, although attention to hygiene is much better, the perfume industry is thriving and worth millions of dollars a year. French perfumes are considered the best in the world, and they are exported to more than one hundred countries.

The town of Grasse in the south of France has been the center of the perfume industry since the sixteenth century. At that time, Grasse was also a center for leather tanning. It became the perfume capital of the world when Catherine de Médicis, queen of France, set the fashion for scented leather gloves. Today, the leather tanneries are gone, but the forty perfume houses founded in the eighteenth and nineteenth centuries are still in business.

Grasse is surrounded by field upon field of flowers: lavender, mimosa, rose, orange blossom, ylang-ylang, and jasmine. The

Below: **Row upon row of lavender flowers. Growing and harvesting flowers is a very tedious occupation. No machine is used in the fields; the flowers are so delicate that automation would destroy them.**

flowers are handpicked, and it may take a group of workers one whole hour to pick 15 pounds (7 kg) of roses. Harvesting jasmine flowers is even more time-consuming: one hour for 1 pound (0.5 kg) of flowers. To pick the flowers, the workers have to be in the fields by 5:00 a.m.

A perfume is made from a combination of essences, extracts of flowers, or other natural sources. Some perfumes require as many as three hundred essences. The blending of essences in exact quantities is the most important step; it gives life to a perfume. The person who creates a perfume is called a "nose." Noses are experts who can identify one scent from six thousand smells with just one whiff. Very few people have the ability to become a nose, and those who do have it are highly sought after in the perfume industry.

It takes thousands of flowers to make a drop of essence. One ton of roses yields only 4 pounds (1.8 kg) of essence. Various methods are used to extract essence from flowers; all are very painstaking: steam distillation, extraction by volatile solvents, or *enfleurage* (ahn-fluh-RAHGE). The last method is used for expensive or potent essences. Pungent blossoms are layered with fats for several months until the fat has absorbed all the aroma of the flowers. Then the oils are "washed" out with alcohol. When the alcohol evaporates, it leaves the pure perfume essence behind.

Saving the Earth

The Green Movement

The green movement started in France in the 1960s. French ecologists fight on many fronts: they protest nuclear proliferation, campaign against uranium mining, stop highway projects, highlight chemical pollution, and demonstrate against any building that threatens the landscape. They urge town councils to recycle their refuse, promote organic farming, preserve wildlife, lobby against hunting, and even organize an annual anti-automobile show.

Swimming with the Fish

The most famous ecologist in France was Jacques-Yves Cousteau (1910–1997). Even as a child, Cousteau was fascinated by water. As an officer in the French Navy, Cousteau started exploring the ocean and developed his love for marine life. One of his earliest achievements was the invention, in 1943, of the Aqualung, the breathing apparatus that enables scuba divers to remain

Left: Jacques-Yves Cousteau loved the ocean and the marvels it contained. He published several books, including *The Silent World*, and made many films about his explorations.

Left: Scuba divers owe their mobility to Cousteau. Cousteau wanted to be able to swim like a fish, moving effortlessly through the water. He invented the Aqualung, a cylinder of air that a diver could carry with him or her. Until then, divers had worn heavy, lead-soled boots and walked on the sea bed, carrying their air hoses behind them.

underwater for several hours. In 1948, Cousteau purchased the ship *Calypso,* and started his incredible work on underwater plants and animals. He began by exploring the Mediterranean and the Red seas, but he also took his ship to the Pacific Ocean, to North America, and to African waters. He produced numerous films and books, increasing public awareness of the underwater world and opening the world of diving to many. For eight years, starting in 1968, the weekly television series, *The Undersea World of Jacques Cousteau,* introduced a world of dolphins, sharks, whales, coral reefs, and sunken treasures to a wide public. Viewers were amazed by the life under the water and became aware of the fragility of this world.

As Cousteau became aware of the increasing destruction of the oceans by pollution and overfishing, he became an avid environmentalist. In 1973, he founded the nonprofit Cousteau Society, which aims to protect ocean life and educate the public. Jacques-Yves Cousteau was awarded the Medal of Freedom by U.S. president Ronald Reagan in 1985.

Tour de France

Racing Against Time

One of the highlights of the year is the Tour de France, a cross-country bicycle race. Since 1903, when the first Tour took place, this grueling race has attracted the best cyclists in the world every year.

The idea for a round-the-country race came from a publisher who wanted to increase the sales of his newspaper. The first Tour departed on July 1, 1903, with seventy-six competitors. The Tour started and ended in Paris, totaling 1,517 miles (2,440 km). At the end of eighteen days, only twenty-one cyclists were left. The winner was Maurice Garin, nicknamed "the little chimney sweeper." He was a favorite with the crowd. Garin was in the lead by two hours and forty-nine minutes at the end of the Tour, a record that still stands.

Today, the Tour is longer and much more taxing. There is only one day's rest for the duration of the race. For three weeks in July, the best cyclists in the world race more than 2,400 miles (3,862 km). The cyclist in the lead at the end of each day wears a yellow jersey. Along the route of the Tour, hundreds of thousands of cycling fans follow the racers. Many more fans around the world follow the race through live television and radio coverage. Many of the racers are foreigners; American Greg LeMond won the Tour three times, in 1986, 1989, and 1990.

Above: **Tour de France cyclists race through the countryside of France, through towns and over steep mountain roads. Each racer belongs to a team of nine riders. The race finally ends on the Champs Elysées in Paris, where thousands of spectators await the cyclists.**

Tour de France Heroes

For the French public, the hero of the Tour de France will always be Jacques Anquetil. Hailing from Normandy, Anquetil won the Tour five times in the 1950s and 1960s. He so dominated the race that, in 1961, he wore the leader's yellow jersey from the beginning to the end.

Another five-time winner was Belgian Eddy Merckx, nicknamed "the cannibal" for making a clean sweep of all titles in 1969. Frenchman Bernard Hinault also won the Tour five times. He was nicknamed "the badger" because he never gave up.

In the 1990s, the Tour was dominated by Spaniard Miguel Indurain, who won the Tour consecutively from 1991 to 1995, a feat never before achieved. Because of his reserve and nonchalance in front of the press, a European newspaper gave him the label "the extraterrestrial."

Left: Biking is not just for champions. Many French adults and children also enjoy mountain biking and exploring the countryside and national parks.

Wild Horses, Flamingos, and Gypsies

Left: The most spectacular birds of the Camargue are the flamingos. The lagoons turn into a sea of pink every spring and summer when these birds arrive from their wintering sites in Africa. Two and a half months later, after hatching and raising their young, the flamingos return to Africa.

The Marshlands of Camargue

The Camargue consists of 367 square miles (950 square km) of marshlands at the mouth of the Rhône River where it flows into the Mediterranean Sea. This area is the deep south of France and does not resemble any other region in the country. The Camargue has its own distinctive flora and fauna, and the local residents have traditions that date back thousands of years.

Designated a botanical and zoological nature reserve in 1927, the Camargue has a unique collection of plants, such as tamarisk trees, narcissus, reeds, wildflowers, and junipers. The dunes and wetlands support a variety of birds, such as eagles, hawks, harriers, herons, kingfishers, and owls. The local white horses are small and sturdy. They have a dark coat when young that turns white by the age of five. Used for riding, these horses roam freely in the wild the rest of the time. Camargue bulls are used in bullfights. The aim of the bullfight in the Camargue is to pluck red rosettes from between a bull's horns with a small hook.

Herding cattle and keeping traditions alive are the *gardians* (gar-DIAHN), the equivalent of American cowboys. They still live in traditional thatched huts and show off their fine horsemanship during festivals and other displays.

SALT OF THE SEA

The production of salt in Camargue has a long history. It was started by the Greeks and the Romans who colonized the region. In September, seawater is pumped into salt pans and left to evaporate. By the following autumn, the salt crystals are ready to be harvested. They are heaped into shimmering mountains called camelles (kah-MELL), which can rise up to 26 feet (8.5 m) high.

A Gypsy Capital

Gypsies from all over Europe converge on the small Camargue town of Saintes-Maries-de-la-Mer (Saint Marys of the Sea) for several days a year each May. This pilgrimage is in honor of Sarah, the patron saint of Gypsies, who is said to have come to the Camargue after being driven out of Palestine in the year A.D. 40.

The celebration lasts two days. Dressed in colorful costumes and carrying a statue of Sarah, the Gypsies observe a candlelight vigil, then march in a procession from the church of Saintes-Maries to the sea. There, they immerse the statue of Sarah in the water and send little paper boats containing a flickering flame out into the sea.

The festival also includes a blessing of horses, parades of gardians and Provençal women in traditional costumes, horse races, and bullfights. Famous Gypsy entertainers are also present, and people start to dance and clap to the rhythms. Dominated by the sound of strumming guitars, Saintes-Maries-de-la-Mer is truly the Gypsy capital of the world.

Below: Gypsies carry statues of Saint Mary Salome and Saint Mary Jacobe to the sea during a festival. These two saints of Biblical times were forced to leave Palestine and were guided to France by Sarah, the patron saint of Gypsies.

RELATIONS WITH NORTH AMERICA

The United States, Canada, and France have been allies for most of North American history since European settlement. Although France was a colonial power on the North American continent, the North American people did not have to fight the French government to gain their freedom. New France in Canada was handed over to the British in 1763 as a result of fighting between France and Britain. Louisiana, also a French territory, was sold to the United States in 1803 for 15 million dollars.

Opposite: **The unmistakable symbol of America — the Statue of Liberty in New York Harbor — was actually a gift from the French. It was shipped over in 1885, and commemorates the friendship of the people of France and the United States.**

The United States, Canada, and France have mutually supported each other in the course of history. French troops helped American patriots win independence from Britain, and American and Canadian soldiers liberated France from German occupation during World Wars I and II. Today, France and North America belong to several international organizations and lend each other support in many world affairs. France and Canada continue to enjoy a special relationship because of France's historical involvement with Canada. France also has a very cordial relationship with Quebec and its prime minister.

Above: **Nova Scotia, originally called Acadia, is on the Atlantic coast of Canada. The first French settlement was established in Nova Scotia in 1605. Today, one-eighth of the people are descended from the French. Many of the rest are of British descent or are descendants of the original Micmac Indians.**

French Settlers in North America

One of the first French explorers in North America was Jacques Cartier, whose first voyage took place in 1534. He led three expeditions altogether, sighting Newfoundland and St. Lawrence Bay. He claimed this area as New France for his king, Francis I. One group of islands discovered by Cartier is still in French hands today: Saint Pierre and Miquelon in the Atlantic Ocean.

Although Cartier made friends with the native populations and was a talented explorer, he did not found any settlements in North America. The honor for this goes to Samuel de Champlain, who made twelve voyages to what is now Canada. On his first trip he followed the St. Lawrence River as far as the Lachine Rapids above Montreal. Later, he explored Nova Scotia and New England and charted the coastline. Champlain's main interest in New France was the lucrative fur trade, but since his king wanted to claim the North American territories for France, he was persuaded to start a colony in exchange for a fur trade permit. The first settlement was at Port Royal (now Annapolis Royal, Nova Scotia), in eastern Canada. Champlain wisely signed peace treaties with the native people, and they taught him many survival skills. Thanks to his and later explorers' close cooperation with the natives, France built a thriving fur trading business in North America.

Above: **Samuel de Champlain (1567–1635) explored much of eastern Canada and New England as well as the Great Lakes.**

Above: **Robert de La Salle (1643–1687) set out from France as a young man to seek his fortune in North America. He was the first to explore the Mississippi and Illinois rivers and claimed the Mississippi Basin for France.**

Left: **Jacques Cartier on the summit of Mount Real.**

76

As the fur trade grew, other explorers gained the courage to explore farther west. Many of them were Catholic priests. One of them, Father Jacques Marquette, explored the Mississippi River with fur trader Louis Joliet. In 1681, Robert de La Salle rowed all the way down the river to the Gulf of Mexico. He claimed the entire Mississippi River valley for France, naming it *Louisiana* in honor of King Louis XIV.

Both the New France and Louisiana settlements were initially populated by hunters and fur trappers. They made an uneasy truce with the Natchez Indians in Louisiana but eventually drove them away to the swamps of Alabama and Georgia.

The early French settlements were sparsely populated because very few French women came to America. The colonizers were adventurers who had no intention of settling down. They were fur traders, priests, and soldiers, not farmers. Many of them married Indian women but eventually went back to France. Their children, of French and Indian parentage, were called *métis* (may-TISS).

Despite the initial reluctance of many French people to settle on the American continent, they were the first colonizers to realize that North America, not France, was their home. French Canadians started calling themselves "Canadians" long before the English-speaking residents of the country did, and even before the country's independence.

Above: **A map of New France, Canada, by Champlain, dating to 1613. This French colony included the shores of the St. Lawrence River, Newfoundland, and Nova Scotia (Acadia), and later extended to the Great Lakes and farther west. When the French lost the battle of the Plains of Abraham to the British, the territory was ceded to Britain.**

Quebec, Center of French Canada

Quebec City was founded by Samuel de Champlain in 1608. As the capital of New France, this fortified city was an important center of trade and development. Today, it is regarded as the cradle of French civilization in America and, in 1985, was named a World Heritage City by the United Nations Educational, Scientific, and Cultural Organization (UNESCO), an agency created in 1946 to promote international relations. Quebec City is still the administrative capital of Quebec province, while Montreal is the economic capital of Quebec. More than three million Quebeckers live in Montreal and its suburbs.

At the outset, Quebec was the center of French-English rivalry in America. Quebec City fell to British forces in 1759 at the end of the Seven Years' War between France and Britain, and France ceded Quebec to Britain in the 1763 Treaty of Paris. Later, the French character of the population was recognized by the Quebec Act of 1774, which granted official recognition to French civil laws, guaranteed religious freedom, and authorized the use of the French language. Today, out of a total population of seven million, more than five million people in Quebec are of French origin. French is one of the official languages of Canada. All public writing in Quebec, such as shop signs and road directions, must be in French.

Above: Quebec City, founded by Samuel de Champlain, is the oldest city in Canada. It has retained a European atmosphere, and the majority of its population speaks French.

SEPARATION FROM CANADA?

Quebeckers are deeply conscious of their historical roots and of their difference from the rest of Canada. Support for independence has grown in the 1990s.

Marquis de Lafayette

One Frenchman whose name is dear to the American people is Marquis de Lafayette. Wealthy and well connected in the French court, Lafayette was a man of great military genius. His first introduction to America came when, as a young man, he was told about the struggles for independence in the American colonies. He bought a ship and, together with several young French military officers, set sail in 1777 to help the Americans fight the British.

Lafayette was immediately welcomed by the Americans. Since he served as a volunteer and had no other motive than to help, Congress made him a major general. Later, he met General George Washington, and the two men struck up a friendship that would last until Washington's death. After two years in North America, Lafayette went back to France to persuade the king to send troops and additional supplies to the Americans. In 1780, he returned to America with supplies and twelve battalions of infantry to fight on the side of the patriots.

Left: **Marquis de Lafayette and George Washington. This great friend of America once wrote to Washington: "Serving America is to my heart an inexpressible happiness." He fought at Valley Forge with Washington and was fiercely loyal to the American leader. His efforts were invaluable during the American War of Independence.**

Louisiana

The territory of Louisiana initially included the whole of the Mississippi River basin. As France, Britain, and Spain battled for power in Europe, Spain won the territory in 1762. It remained Spanish for nearly forty years but was returned to France when Spain began to decline. In 1803, Napoleon Bonaparte sold the whole territory to the United States (the Louisiana Purchase), doubling the size of the country. Thirteen states or parts of states were carved out of the Louisiana territory: Louisiana, Arkansas, Missouri, Iowa, North Dakota, South Dakota, Nebraska, Kansas, Wyoming, Minnesota, Oklahoma, Colorado, and Montana.

Louisiana was first settled by adventurers, French troops, convicts, and runaway slaves. The French came from several directions. Many came in 1755 after they were expelled from New France by the British. These settlers were called Acadians since they came from Acadia (Nova Scotia today) in Canada. The name *Acadian* was later corrupted into *Cajun* and is still used today.

JAMBALAYA AND GUMBO

Creole and Cajun cuisine have contributed to the fame of New Orleans as a melting pot of French and American culture. Both cuisines use the sausages and smoked meats that are a staple in French cuisine, and the tomatoes, onions, and garlic favored in Mediterranean cooking. Gumbo, jambalaya, and blackened fish are typical dishes.

Political Allies

France has had strong ties with the United States and Canada for many years. U.S. and Canadian troops were part of the Allied Forces that helped the French defeat the Germans in World War I. Their contribution was even greater in World War II, when Germany occupied France. Thousands of U.S. troops took part in the D-Day landing that contributed to the end of the war. On June 6, 1944, Allied Forces landed on several beaches in Normandy and swiftly proceeded to defeat the Germans. U.S. troops landed on the western beaches of Utah and Omaha, while British, Canadian, and French soldiers landed at Gold, Juno, and Sword. These beaches are still called by their code names.

After World War II, a number of European countries, including France, joined the United States and Canada to form an alliance for collective defense. The North Atlantic Treaty Organization (NATO) has sixteen members today. The organization now acts as an ally of the United States in confrontations everywhere in the world. France, however, has had an ambivalent relationship with NATO since the days of General de Gaulle. Even though it was one of the founding members, France has steadfastly refused to allow NATO forces to be stationed on French soil. De Gaulle pulled the country out of NATO, but subsequent leaders reversed that decision.

Above: **The American cemetery at Omaha Beach in Normandy, France, is for soldiers who lost their lives during World War II.**

Opposite: **New Orleans, capital of Louisiana, has become famous for its jazz music. This city is where French influence is most apparent in the United States. Most streets and public places have retained their French colonial names, and local delicacies include** *beignets* **(bay-NYAY), a donut without a hole, and** *boudin* **(boo-DAN), a sausage filled with meat and rice.**

Trade

France enjoys healthy trade relations with the United States and Canada. French exports to the United States include foodstuffs, telecommunications equipment, and machinery. France's imports include crude oil and industrial equipment. The G7 trade grouping was born on French soil, with the first summit taking place at Rambouillet in 1975. In addition to France and the United States, this group includes Canada, Britain, Germany, Japan, and Italy. It also meets with Russia and the European Union. Its purpose is to improve trade and the world economy. As a leading world power, the United States is a major voice in the grouping. France, on the other hand, is more individualistic and complies with summit agreements to a lesser degree than the other G7 members.

Cultural Exchanges and Fashion

In addition exchanging goods, France and the United States also exchange their know-how with each other, and specialized people work in each other's country. Hollywood and American cinema, for example, have greatly benefited from the work of top French directors Louis Malle and Luc Besson. Since they share the language, some French people move to Quebec to work.

For many decades now, France has set fashion trends for the rest of the world. American designers and buyers are still influenced by the great French fashion houses started by Coco Chanel, Yves Saint-Laurent, and Christian Dior, but talented American designers have also expanded the creative scope of French fashion houses. For example, well-established luggage house Louis Vuitton has found a new direction and renewed sales with American Marc Jacobs leading its design team.

The most lasting French influence on American fashion is, ironically, the humble and ubiquitous denim jeans. The word *denim* is a contraction of *de Nîmes*, meaning a type of cloth made in the town of Nîmes in the south of France. Denim was introduced in the United States in the 1850s by German-born businessman Levi Strauss. His sturdy work pants made from denim material soon became very popular with students, working people, and children. After World War II, denim jeans made their way to Europe, and today, most French people consider the garment to be the epitome of American culture, even though the cloth originated in their own country.

Above: **A model for Yves Saint-Laurent, the French fashion designer. Paris is a leader in fashion design, and designers all over the world follow the latest styles in French fashion.**

Trends

Like most other places, American-style fast food and pop music have made it to France. Many in France disapprove and say they are victims of American mass culture and consumerism. Although shunned by all well-to-do French people, American burger chains draw large crowds of teenagers, tourists, and the less well-off. Hamburgers have also made their way into home cooking. French children love their *steak hâché* (steck a-CHAY) with French fries and ketchup. They also like to drink *coca*, or cola drinks.

A French extremist group, called the Joyous Anti Fast-Food Network, has been kidnapping statues of Ronald McDonald from restaurant shop fronts. According to this group, the statue represents the undesirable invasion of American fast food. Their main objective is to defend traditional French cooking.

The influence of French cuisine on American food however, has been better appreciated. Creole cuisine in New Orleans, Louisiana, was the creation of the French and Spanish settlers and their black servants, and it is greatly enjoyed.

Below: **Planet Hollywood is just one of many American chains that has made it to Paris.**

Americans in France

France has always held much attraction for Americans, who see it as the epitome of elegance and refinement. During the nineteenth and early twentieth centuries, wealthy Americans completed their education with a "grand tour" of Europe. They always spent more time in France than anywhere else, visiting museums and shopping in the high-fashion houses. Americans who took up residence in France were mainly writers, philosophers, and artists. They benefited enormously from the intellectual and artistic freedom in the country but also contributed much to the writing and music scene. Musicians Sidney Bechet and Dizzy Gillespie, for example, introduced jazz to the French public.

Josephine Baker, from St. Louis, Missouri, was the undisputed music-hall queen of Paris in the 1920s. She made her debut at the famous Folies Bergères in 1925, "clad only in a tutu made of rhinestone-studded bananas and three bracelets." Josephine Baker introduced the Charleston to Parisians, while fellow American Duke Ellington popularized American jazz. Baker worked for the French Resistance during World War II, for which she was awarded the most prestigious military decorations in France, the Croix de Guerre and the Legion of Honor.

Below: **Ernest Hemingway** *(left)* **and Gertrude Stein** *(right)* **were among the American writers living in Paris in the 1920s. Hemingway's book,** *A Moveable Feast***, a portrayal of bohemian life in Paris between the two world wars, evokes the unique experience of these renowned people.**

Above: **A jazz band in Rouen, France.**

Jazz

Jazz is the most important American musical import in France. Since the 1920s, when great American jazz musicians, such as Duke Ellington, performed to packed houses in Paris, jazz has been popular with French music lovers. There are several jazz festivals a year throughout France. They draw the best in the industry, and listeners come from all over Europe. The most well known is the Antibes Jazz Festival in the south, started in 1960. All the famous jazz musicians have performed at Antibes, including Ray Charles and Miles Davis (who made their debut there), Louis Armstrong, and Ella Fitzgerald.

Cajun Music

In the United States, Cajun folk music and zydeco still retain a strong French influence. Cajun songs are sung in the Cajun dialect, a form of French laced with Indian, Spanish, German, English, and African expressions. The sound of the fiddle is very strong in Cajun music, and the style is enjoying a revival. Zydeco is a mixture of Cajun and African sounds. Forsaking the fiddle, zydeco uses the saxophone or trumpet, cowbells, and an instrument called a *frottoir* (froh-TWAR), which is a modified washboard.

FRANCE

ENGLAND
NORTH SEA
NETHERLANDS
BELGIUM
LUXEMBOURG
Strait of Dover

Lille
NORD-PAS-DE-CALAIS

Amiens
PICARDIE

English Channel
Le Havre
UPPER NORMANDY
Rouen
Seine
Reims
LORRAINE
Strasbour

Caen
LOWER NORMANDY
Versailles
PARIS
ÎLE-DE-FRANCE
Marne
CHAMPAGNE-ARDENNE
Domrémy

Mont-Saint-Michel
Couesnon

Brest
Quimper
BRITTANY (BRETAGNE)

PAYS DE LA LOIRE
Orléans
CENTRE
Dijon
FRANCHE-COMTÉ

VOSGES MOUNTAINS

Loire
BURGUNDY (BOURGOGNE)
Saône

ATLANTIC OCEAN
Nantes

Lake Geneva
JURA MOUNTAINS

POITOU-CHARENTES
LIMOUSIN
Limoges
Vichy
Lyon
Mont Blanc (15,771 ft, 4,805 m)

Bay of
Biscay
AUVERGNE
Massif Central
RHÔNE-ALPES
A L P S

Bordeaux
AQUITAINE
Garonne
CÉVENNES
Rhône
PROVENCE-ALPES CÔTE-D'AZUR

Gulf of Gascogne

MIDI-PYRÉNÉES
Avignon
Montpellier
LUBERON HILLS
Grasse
Nie
Cannes

Toulouse
Marseille
Saint-Tropez

Lourdes
P Y R E N E E S
LANGUEDOC-ROUSSILLON
Camargue
Saintes-Maries-de-la-Mer
French Riviera

Golfe du Lion

ANDORRA
MEDITERRANEAN SEA

SPAIN

Legend	
———	State Boundary
- - -	Tropic of Capricorn
■	Capital
●	City
～	River

N

GERMANY

ALSACE

SWITZERLAND

ITALY

MONACO

CORSICA
(France)

Alps D4
Alsace E2
Amiens C2
Andorra C5
Aquitaine B4
Atlantic Ocean A3
Auvergne C4
Avignon D4

Bay of Biscay A4
Belgium D1
Bordeaux B4
Brest A2
Brittany (Bretagne) A2
Burgundy (Bourgogne)
    C3–D3

Caen B2
Camargue D5
Cannes D4
Centre C3
Cévennes C4
Champagne-Ardenne
    C2–D2
Corsica E5
Couesnon River B2

Dijon D3
Domrémy D2

England B1
English Channel A2

Franche-Comté D3
French Riviera D5

Garonne River B4
Geneva, Lake D3
Germany E1
Golfe du Lion C5–D5
Grasse D4
Gulf of Gascogne A4

Île-de-France C2
Italy E4

Jura Mountains D3

Languedoc-Roussillon
    C5
Le Havre B2
Lille C1
Limoges C3
Limousin C3
Loire River B3
Lorraine D2
Lourdes B5
Lower Normandy B2
Luberon Hills D4
Luxembourg D1–D2
Lyon D3

Marne River C2

Above: Fountain at Versailles, palace of the Sun King.

Marseille D5
Massif Central C4
Mediterranean Sea D5
Midi-Pyrénées B4–C4
Monaco E4
Mont Blanc D3
Mont-Saint-Michel B2
Montpellier C4

Nantes B3
Netherlands D1
Nice E4
Nord-Pas-de-Calais C1
Normandy B2
North Sea C1

Orléans C2

Paris C2
Pays de la Loire B2–B3
Picardie C2
Poitou-Charentes B3
Provence-Alpes-Côte-
    d'Azur D4
Pyrenees B5

Quimper A2

Reims C2
Rhine River E2
Rhône-Alpes D4
Rhône River D4
Rouen C2

Saint-Tropez D5
Saintes-Maries-de-la-
    Mer D5
Saône River D3
Seine River C2
Spain A5
Strait of Dover C1
Strasbourg E2
Switzerland E3

Toulouse C5

Upper Normandy B2–C2

Versailles C2
Vichy C3
Vosges Mountains D2

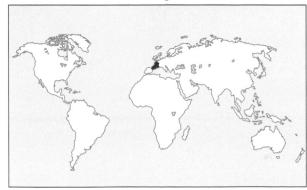

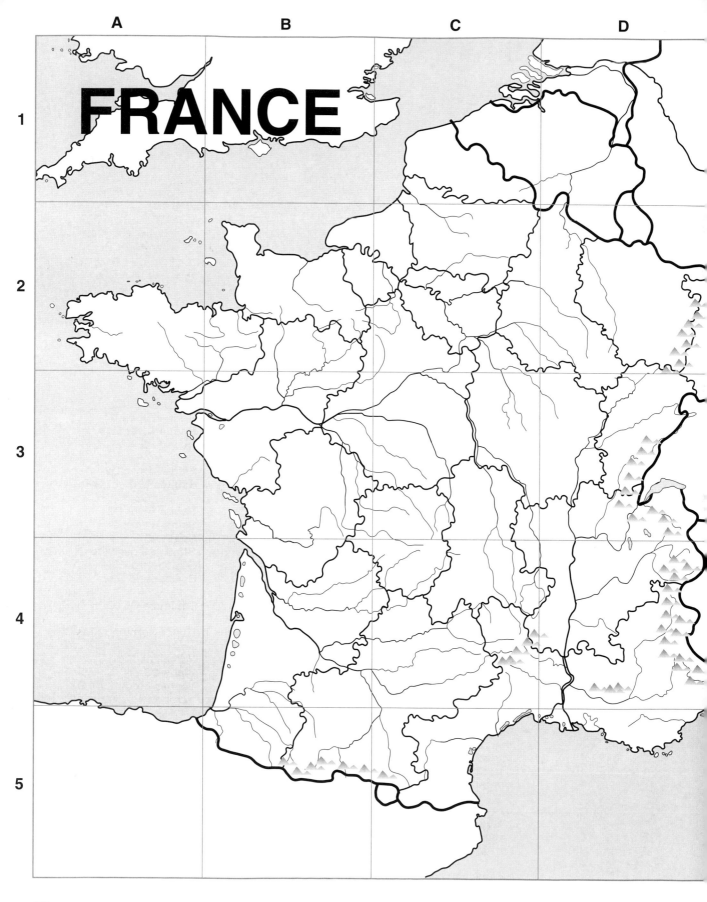

FRANCE

E

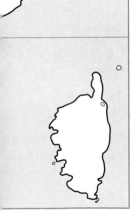

How Is Your Geography?

Learning to identify the main geographical areas and points of a country can be challenging. Although it may seem difficult at first to memorize the location and spelling of major cities or the names of mountain ranges, rivers, deserts, lakes, and other prominent physical features, the end result of this effort can be very rewarding. Places you previously did not know existed will suddenly come to life when referred to in world news, whether in newspapers, television reports, or other books and reference sources. This knowledge will make you feel a bit closer to the rest of the world, with its fascinating variety of cultures and physical geography.

Used in a classroom setting, the instructor can make duplicates of this map using a copy machine (PLEASE DO NOT WRITE IN THIS BOOK!). Students can then fill in any requested information on their individual map copies. Used one-on-one, the student can also make copies of the map on a copy machine and use them as a study tool. The student can practice identifying place names and geographical features on his or her own.

Above: An ancient Roman aqueduct in Provence.

France at a Glance

Official Name	The French Republic
Capital	Paris
Official Language	French
Population	58 million
Land Area	212,742 square miles (551,000 square kilometers)
Regions	Alsace, Aquitaine, Auvergne, Burgundy, Brittany, Champagne-Ardenne, Centre, Corsica, Franche-Comté, Île-de-France, Languedoc-Roussillon, Limousin, Lorraine, Lower Normandy, Midi-Pyrénées, Nord-Pas-de-Calais, Pays de la Loire, Picardie, Poitou-Charentes, Provence-Alpes-Côte d'Azur, Rhône-Alpes, Upper Normandy, overseas departments and territories
Highest Point	Mont Blanc (15,771 feet/4,805 meters)
Longest River	Loire River (634 miles/1,020 kilometers)
Main Religion	Roman Catholicism
National Anthem	La Marseillaise
National Motto	Liberty, equality, fraternity
National Emblem	Cockerel
Festivals	New Year (January), Carnival (February), Easter (March/April), La Bravade (May), Les Saintes (May), Avignon (July), Lourdes Pilgrimage (August), Vendanges (September), Christmas (December)
Anniversaries	Labor Day (May 1), VE Day (May 8), Bastille Day (July 14), Remembrance Day (November 11)
Famous Leaders	Charlemagne (742–814), Joan of Arc (1412–1431), Louis XIV (1638–1715), Napoleon Bonaparte (1769–1821), Charles de Gaulle (1890–1970)
Currency	Francs (FF 6 = U.S. $1 as of 1998)

Opposite: **Hotel de Vogüé. Many rooftops in Dijon have beautiful tilework.**

Glossary

French Vocabulary

baguette (ba-GET): long, thin loaf of bread.

Beurs (BURR): people of North African ancestry living in France.

bouillabaisse (boo-yah-BES): stew of fish, tomatoes, wine, and olive oil.

boules (BOOL): a type of lawn bowling.

brasserie (brass-REE): informal restaurant.

café au lait (ka-fay oh LAY): coffee with a generous dose of milk.

camelle (kah-MELL): heap of sea salt.

cochonnet (ko-cho-NAY): the small ball used as a target in the game of *boules* or *pétanque*.

coiffe (KWAF): lace headdress that is part of the traditional women's costume in Brittany.

collége (kol-EHJ): secondary school.

enfleurage (ahn-fluh-RAHGE): a technique used in the perfume industry. Flowers are layered with fats that absorb the fragrance and are then removed.

foie gras (fwa GRAH): the fattened liver of goose or duck, a delicacy from southwestern France

gardian (gar-DIAHN): the equivalent of the American cowboy in the south of France.

La Francophonie (LAH fran-ko-fo-NEE): grouping of French-speaking countries.

lycée (li-SAY): last three years of schooling before baccalaureate exams.

maison bloc (may-zohn BLOC): style of farmhouse in which the house and outbuildings share the same roof.

métis (may-TISS): people of French and Indian heritage.

miquelots (mi-KE-loh): pilgrims to the abbey of Mont-Saint-Michel.

mistral (miss-TRAHL): a cold, dry wind that blows in spring in Provence.

pain au chocolat (pehn o sho-ko-LAH): a flaky pastry baked with a bar of chocolate in the middle.

pardon (pahr-DOHN): ceremony performed on a saint's day in Brittany to grant pardon for people's sins.

pétanque (pay-TAHNK): a form of lawn bowling that is very popular in the south of France. The balls are thrown in the air toward the target rather than rolled along the ground as in boules.

tartine (tar-TEEN): slice of bread covered with butter, jam, cheese, or honey.

tu (TEU): you, the informal pronoun.

vendanges (vahn-DAHNJE): the harvesting of wine grapes in September.

vous (VOO): you, the formal pronoun.

English Vocabulary

abbey: a monastery with an abbot as head.

abdicated: to give up or renounce the throne or other high office.

aristocracy: the upper class; the nobility.

baccalaureate: equivalent to high school graduation, for which students must take difficult exams.

benchmark: a standard by which other items can be measured.

bourgeoisie: the middle class.

Breton: the term for the people, culture, and language of Brittany, a region in northwestern France.

cassock: the long coat, usually black, worn by a priest.

Celts: an ancient people that migrated into France. Irish, Welsh, and highland Scots are also of Celtic origin.

cohabitation: a government phenomenon in which the president and prime minister are from different political parties with different ideologies.

commune: a township run by a mayor; the smallest administrative unit in France.

croissant: a flaky French pastry in the shape of a crescent.

Cro-Magnon: the ancestor of modern man in France; lived in about 25,000 B.C.

culminate: end.

druids: medicine men in ancient Celtic society.

effigy: an image or statue of a person.

Enlightenment: an eighteenth-century philosophical movement.

Entente Cordiale: a friendly agreement between nations.

etiquette: the manners required for proper social behavior.

exodus: a large number of people leaving at the same time.

extravagance: a great, unnecessary spending of money.

Franco-Prussian War: the war between France and Prussia (now in Germany) from 1870 to 1871.

Gallic: of ancient Gaul; French.

Gaul: name for ancient France.

grueling: exhausting, very tiring.

guillotine: an execution instrument that beheads the person. It was used primarily during the French Revolution.

hierarchical: a system of ranking according to wealth, class, or status.

Huguenots: French Protestants in the sixteenth and seventeenth centuries.

hydroelectricity: electricity generated from the energy of falling water.

impressionism: a style in painting that tries to capture the immediate impressions of the artist. Impressionism first developed in France in the late nineteenth century.

itinerant: traveling from place to place.

menhir: a tall stone.

Minitel: an online service similar to the Internet.

pasteurization: developed by Louis Pasteur in the nineteenth century, the process of using heat to destroy harmful microorganisms in food, such as milk.

Pyrenean: of the Pyrenees mountain range.

razed: destroyed.

Resistance: the World War II underground movement against the Nazis in France.

spa: a resort facility around mineral springs.

suffragist: a person who works toward extending the vote, especially for women.

taxing: tiring.

Teutonic: of northern European descent.

tricolor: the name for the French flag, which has three colors — blue, white, and red.

troubadours: traveling storytellers in the Middle Ages, who narrated long stories of love and adventure.

ubiquitous: being everywhere.

vigil: staying awake overnight, often for a religious festival.

More Books to Read

Cities at War: Paris. Nathan Aaseng (New Discovery Books)

Claude Debussy. Wendy Thomas (Viking Press)

Discovering France. Jo Sturges (Crestwood House)

France. Country Topics for Craft Projects series. Anita Ganeri and Rachel Wright (Franklin Watts)

France. Festivals of the World series. Susan McKay (Gareth Stevens)

French in America. Virginia Brainard Kurz (Lerner Publications)

The French Revolution. Adrian Gilbert (Thomson Learning)

The Importance of Napoleon Bonaparte. Bob Carroll (Lucent Books)

The Inside-Outside Book of Paris. Roxie Munro (Dutton Children's Books)

Joan of Arc. Tracy Christopher (Chelsea House Publishers)

Louis XIV. David L. Smith (Cambridge University Press)

Passport to France. Dominique Norbrook (Franklin Watts)

Videos

Discovering France. (International Video Network)

Paris: City of Light. (V.I.E.W. Video)

Touring France. (Questar Video)

Web Sites

sunsite.sut.ac.jp/wm/paint/theme/impressionnisme.html

sunsite.sut.ac.jp/wm/paris/

moltenlava.com/uo/Celtichistory.html

www.france.diplomatie.fr/france/index.gb.html

www.mmmpce.org/jerrywalkosz/joan.htm

Due to the dynamic nature of the Internet, some web sites stay current longer than others. To find additional web sites, use a reliable search engine with one or more of the following keywords to help you locate information about France. Keywords: *France, French, Gaul, Impressionism, Napoleon, Paris.*

Index